GLIMPSES OF NINEVEH.

B. C. 690.

NEW YORK:
MILLER & CURTIS, 321 BROADWAY,
SUCCESSORS TO DIX, EDWARDS & CO.
1857.

Miller & Curtis,
Printers and Stereotypers, N. Y.

CONTENTS.

GLIMPSES OF NINEVEH.

B.C. 690.

LETTER I.

TELASSAR AT NINEVEH TO MEMUCAN AT BABYLON.

This is the fifteenth day, my dear friend, since your departure, and we are hourly expecting tidings from you. I should have written you ere this, according to our agreement, but, truth to say, my hours have been quite too crowded with cares and duties, to admit of it. Every day, indeed, since you left, have I been in attendance at the palace till sunset, drafting decrees, sealing dispatches, transcribing and collating state papers without number; while, at home, as you are aware, the condition of my beloved wife has been such as to leave me no thought for other matters. Mylitta be praised though, her perils are past; early yesterday morning, she was delivered of a son; as pretty a babe, though I say it, as ever gladdened a fond father's heart. The stars, too, are propitious, and if I read aright their shining page, the young Memucan (for so, my dear friend, we are to name him, in your honor) is destined to figure worthily in the future of Assyria. Zeresh, I am happy to say, is rapidly regaining her strength; so much so, that we have set apart the day after to-morrow for our thanksgivings and sacrifices. Before I left home, indeed, this morning, your kinsman, the excellent Zothar, had sent us a votive lamb to grace our festival—the flower of his fold, and the most exquisite little creature I ever beheld—led in triumph, too, most appropriately, by that sweetest of Nineveh's damsels, the darling Nitocris.

I have another piece of good news which I am sure will gratify you. You must know, then, that his most sacred majesty was graciously pleased, a few days since, to confer upon me the appointment of first scribe in waiting, and chief keeper of the archive chamber; nay, more, sent for me in person, and, after some words of approbation of my past services, with his own royal hands, invested me with the robe and ring of office. Need I tell you, dear Memucan, how overjoyed I have been at such a mark of favor, or with what grateful zeal I have entered on my new duties! I have since heard that my name was suggested to his majesty, by our revered Archimagus himself, and am happy in the thought that the selection is, almost without exception, acceptable to the members of the sacred college.

You well know, my friend, how arduous, how multiform are the labors of this, to me so unexpected, station; what precious treasures are intrusted to my keeping; what weighty secrets of state I am called to partake in; what documents to compose, transcribe, epitomize; what returns to examine, consultations to attend, orders to give, labors of others to supervise. Oh, may the gods grant me health and heart faithfully to perform all these things, and to find favor, ever as now, in the eyes of Sennacherib our king!

To-day I have finished, and put into the hands of the engravers, the "Palace Journal" for the month just past; and, in a few days more, will have prepared the accustomed summary, for the month previous. A few reports are still due from the governors and commissioners of some of the more distant provinces, but they are momently expected. Enough have been received, however, whereon to base a fair estimate of the resources and condition of the empire. The result is, indeed, most gratifying, most auspicious. The huge columns of figures that set it forth, formidable as they appear to the aching fingers of scribes, yet must thrill the heart of our good king with rapture. Never, never before was Assyria so prosperous—never sate monarch on a throne so glorious as ours. All is peace, too, and obedience, among our tributaries (with one single exception), from Sardis even unto the Caspian, from Pontus to the furthest corner of Arabia. At home, too, what evidences of wealth and prosperity! Never, as now, did our fields so respond to the labors of the husbandman; never were our fair rivers so alive with commerce, our marts so thronged with traffickers, our roads so crowded with caravans, our public works so vast and productive, our fortresses so well manned, our armies so large and well-disciplined. Our blessed religion, too; when, ever before, were Assyria's gods so widely and worthily worshiped, their temples so many and gorgeous, their ceremonials so magnificent, their priests so devoted, their altars so laden with victims, their shrines so resplendent with votive offerings, their sacred fires so lovingly tended? What loyal heart does not leap with joy at the thought of all these things? The only dark spot, indeed, in this bright picture, as I have above intimated, is our relations with Armenia. King Milidduris, it would seem, utterly forgetful of the severe lessons of the past, has again given evidence of a contumacious and rebellious spirit, has withheld his customary gifts and tributes, and, at this moment, has no representative at the capital. Two days ago, the Armenian ambassador left the city, in great haste, no leave asked, no vows of homage paid, no respectful message, even, left behind him. His majesty is sorely vexed thereat, and this very morning has a courier been dispatched with a decree, to the dominions of the recusant king. Ten days are, therein, allowed him to repent, and return to his allegiance; failing which—to use the words of the decree itself—he is threatened with a punishment, even more terrible than that inflicted on his rebellious father, by the divine Sargon. It is thought that an armed force will yet be necessary to recall the traitor to his senses, so mischievous are the counsels that prevail at his court. In that event, however, the king will not go, in person, against the rebels, but the command of the troops will be intrusted to our great captain, Rabsaris. His skill, experience, and thorough knowledge of the country will, doubtless, insure a speedy and glorious conclusion to the war.

This reminds me, by the way, that our young friend Meres, the eldest son of the general, has just made his first appearance in military life. He was presented to his majesty a few days since, who was quite pleased with his handsome person, and the intelligence of his replies. He, moreover, had the good fortune to distinguish himself at our last hunt, winning the praises of all, by his admirable horsemanship, and mastery of his weapons; piercing to the heart a young lion, at a moment of peril—so his father was telling me, this very morning—with an address and intrepidity that did not escape the royal eye. The king, indeed, presented him, on the spot, with a superbly-embroidered cloak, as a mark of his esteem, and has since given him a lieutenancy in the Royal Guards. I had a glimpse of him, this morning, in his new uniform—well did he become it. A more beautiful and well-appointed young warrior never passed beneath the gates of Nineveh. He is as discreet and virtuous, too, as he is brave. He will probably accompany his father in the expedition against Armenia. But my eyes are weary, and I must reserve the remainder of my epistle for to-morrow.

Another busy day at the palace. In the first place, you must know that the Egyptian ambassadors arrived yesterday, bearing with them the treaty agreed upon, some months since, between the two monarchs. I was summoned at an early hour this morning, to the audience-chamber, for the purpose of reading it to his majesty. The principal clauses in the treaty are to the following effect: King Sabaco renounces forever all claims to territory on the eastern shore of the Red sea; promises to withdraw, at once, his fleet from Phœnicia; binds himself to abstain from all further intervention in the affairs of Syria, or of Judea; and, finally, agrees to pay ten thousand rings of silver, and two thousand bags of gold-dust, into our royal treasury; these being, as you may remember, the identical conditions imposed by his majesty, immediately after the great battle of Ekron; conditions far more lenient, indeed, than those insisted upon, at the close of our last war with Egypt. These terms have, at length, been complied with, the delay in the payment of the money having been occasioned by the rebellion in Ethiopia, and other causes duly recited by the ambassadors, and to the entire satisfaction of his majesty. Immediately after the reading of the document, he was pleased to express his royal assent thereto, and, with characteristic promptness, ordered a copy to be made forthwith. In less than an hour were the papers compared and certified, the seals of their majesties impressed upon the appendant tablets, and the original duly deposited among the archives of the nation.

After the audience, I had the pleasure of a few

moments' conversation with the ambassadors. Most courteous and accomplished gentlemen I found them, and perfect masters of Assyrian. They will remain some days with us, having apartments assigned them in the palace of the Archimagus. One of them was so kind as to be the bearer of an epistle to me, from our young friend, Akbar, at Memphis. You will be pleased to learn that he is in excellent health, and writes in his usual sprightly vein. He has determined to remain another twelvemonth at the capital, to perfect his geometrical and musical studies. Accompanying his letter, was a jar of the far-famed honey of Athrybis, and another for yourself. We have already opened ours, and Zeresh pronounces it the most delicious she ever tasted. I shall forward yours as soon as I learn your address at Babylon. I should have mentioned, by the way, that among the royal gifts brought by the ambassadors, was a magnificent service of porcelain, the admiration of the court. I had a hasty glance at it this morning. There are some fifty pieces in all. Some of the cups especially delighted me, by the marvelous grace and delicacy of their forms, and still more, by the inimitable way in which the colors were blended and harmonized. Such fruit and flower-painting I never beheld. I could have spent the whole day, lingering over their beauties, but their fair images soon disappeared amidst the dry statistics of the archive chamber. Ah, dear, what a world of documents, of all sorts, have I been plodding through since morning! My poor brain is in a whirl at the bare thought of them—reports of commissioners, returns of census-takers, rolls of tax-gatherers, estimates of contractors, deeds, decrees, coast-surveys, astronomical tables, explorations of mines, maps of our new provinces in the west, plans of fortresses, army and navy lists, registers of victims and of offerings, and Belus knows what else besides! Rightly to record the doings of the royal household itself, is no slight task, brother; but how infinitely more arduous is the part of the historiographer! Out of such a mass of varied and complicated materials, monthly to prepare an epitome, which shall be at once comprehensive, accurate, and orderly—an epitome worthy indeed to be inscribed in letters of bronze on pillars of marble, and to meet the eyes of future monarchs—this is a duty, the lofty and responsible nature of which one cannot fitly appreciate till he is called upon to discharge it. Thanks to the kind explanations and aids of my worthy predecessor, which have so materially relieved my labors. In a few days now, they will be completed, and then I may hope for an interval of comparative repose.

To-morrow, leave of absence has been graciously accorded me, for our holiday in honor of the dear young new-comer. As I write, little Semiramis is seated at my feet, her pretty fingers busily employed in weaving the garlands for our feast. Her bright eyes ought to have been quenched in sleep an hour ago, but she pleaded so earnestly for a reprieve, that I could not resist her.

Since you left, the statues intended for the eastern portal of the temple have been raised to their places, and the sculptors are now giving them the finishing touches. They are, indeed, admirable works; the design, expression, proportions, all harmonizing with the magnificent pile which they adorn. The interior has been finished for some time, and, to-morrow, the day of dedication will be duly announced to the people.

I have just been favored with a visit from our voluble neighbor, Menahem, who has been for the last half hour pouring forth a constant stream of small talk—the main theme of his discourse, the prospects of the sesame crop, which he says will be full four-fold greater than ever before known in Assyria. Poor Semiramis was soon put to rest by his eloquence, and it was with great difficulty that I could refrain from following the dear child's example. You ought to be thankful, however, for the interruption, in that it has spared you the addition of another leaf to my already sufficiently voluminous epistle. And so, my dear friend, farewell. Fail not to write often, and to inform us of all that befalls you in your journeyings.

The gods bless and keep you, crown with success your mission, and send you back to us again in health and peace! Such is the constant prayer of your ever-loving TELASSAR

LETTER II.

MEMUCAN TO TELASSAR.

I WROTE you a few lines, some days since, announcing our safe arrival here, and the hearty welcome with which we were greeted by the excellent Adar. So hospitable has he been, indeed, that it was only yesterday that we were permitted to leave his pleasant house, and establish ourselves in lodgings. We have found most commodious and central ones. To describe them more precisely; we occupy the third floor of No. 2017, in the centre of square No. 340, at the intersection of East twelfth and South eleventh streets; the very next door but one, my friend, from the apartments occupied by you, during your last visit here. These last we should have preferred, but they have been for some time in the possession of the Persian ambassador. The family, whose place we are filling, are at present at Ecbatana, where they will probably be compelled to spend the ensuing winter and spring. Our front balconies, as you are aware, command a most superb view, both up and down the river; while, in the rear, we have the privilege of a spacious and charming garden, enlivened by two sprightly fountains, musical with birds, and gay with the flowers of all climes; as delightful a spot for moonlight meditations as student's heart could wish. And then, the picture from our house-top—is it not one that even a Ninevite might fondly linger over? True, I miss our noble back-ground of snow-clad hills, our majestic oak-groves, our vine-yards and our olive-orchards; nor do I see any such magnificent groups of palaces and temples as crown the platforms of our own metropolis; but on the other hand, there is an inexhaustible variety and animation in the scene here; such a stir and bustle in the thronged streets, such an air of enjoyment about the gayly-painted houses, such a confusion of tongues and of costumes in the innumerable market-places of the town, such a ceaseless stream of life passing in and out of its glittering gates, such an accumulation of merchandise from all corners of the earth, such a crowd of vessels of all hues and shapes, enlivening its noble river, as together constitute a panorama most amusing, exciting, and instructive. How different, my dear friend, from the repose and dignity of our own stately Nineveh!

This is our eighth day here, and I begin to feel

already quite like a Chaldean. Thanks to your letters, I have made many pleasant acquaintances, and have been received with uniform courtesy and hospitality. Zethar, too (whose long letter to his kinsman Hegai accompanies this), is enjoying himself exceedingly. The good Adar has taken quite a fancy to him. He has already been with him to see the tunnel, the tower, and the arsenal, and to-morrow proposes to show him all the wonders of the observatory. I wish he had more steadiness of character. One would little suspect, from his mad pranks at times, how much real depth of thought and feeling there is in him. And then, such a dandy! There is not a beau in all Babylon that wears a daintier cloak, or flourishes a more sumptuous walking-stick.

It is, indeed, pleasant to witness the agreeable relations now subsisting between the two cities, as contrasted with those of former days. Peace and good-will everywhere prevail; and though six years have hardly elapsed since the last unhappy rebellion, and its speedy and terrible punishment, not a trace of it seems to survive, either in the appearance of the country, or in the memories of its inhabitants. Not a neglected field or deserted house have I seen, since I left home; while the walls of the city have been restored, and are stronger and loftier than ever;

the canals have all been repaired, and many of them enlarged; the highways are in admirable condition. Of the twelve princely roads that radiate from this great centre of traffic, every one seems alive with travelers. The inns swarm with merchants, the dock-yards with laborers, the temples with priests and devotees; the astrologers are again at their watch-towers, studying the stars more diligently than ever. Everything, indeed, seems to betoken a long career of plenty and prosperity. Thanks to the gods, and to the beneficent sway of the glorious Bel-Adon!

I had the honor of being presented to his majesty, the day before yesterday. He received me most graciously, and promised to give my plans and drawings a thorough inspection. What a noble presence he has! How like, and yet how unlike, his august uncle! The same tall and commanding figure, the same deep and sonorous voice; but oh, how different the expression of the eyes! One can hardly imagine their mild, gentle lustre disturbed by those fierce flashes, that at times make the stoutest quail before Sennacherib; and yet, there is a firmness about that beautiful mouth of his that attests a divine commission to govern. He had time but for a hasty glance over one or two of my designs, and seemed pleased with them. He will, no doubt, announce his decision in a day or two.

As you predicted, the crops of the year have been large beyond all precedent. Both here, and on our journey hither, we have had abundant evidences of the fact. The hay-crop has been perfectly enormous; and so with the wheat, and the barley, and the millet, and the sesame. The cotton, they say, will yield at least three hundred-fold to the planter, and will keep the looms of Babylon busy for many a long month to come. And as to the sugar, I hardly dare tell you what I have witnessed; plantation after plantation, in which the cane had reached the height of twenty to twenty-five feet; immense fields, in whose mazes an army of horsemen might have lost their way. And oh, the palm-groves! One must indeed visit Babylonia, rightly to appreciate the beauty and value of this precious gift of heaven. The other fruits here are not so far inferior to those of Assyria as I had expected, while the vegetables are as excellent as they are abundant. Such colossal beets, and onions, and radishes, and cucumbers never gladdened my eyes before; and as to the melon department, I beheld a water-melon in market, yesterday, that it actually took four slaves to lift, and when it was fairly cut in two at last, the glory of its hues all but rivaled that of a Syrian sunset. What a soil! What a soil!

I need not tell you that we have duly paid our vows at the temple of Belus—almost daily, indeed—since our arrival; nor did we fail to suspend our tablets before the throne of Oannes. The temple disappointed me, I confess, being neither so vast nor splendid as my fancy had painted it. Its sculptures are not to be named with those of the temple of Asshur, nor even of Nisroch; the inscriptions are dingy, in places, almost illegible, and the ceiling sadly needs regilding. On expressing my surprise at this neglect to our friend, Adar, he replied that it was his majesty's intention speedily to demolish the edifice, and to erect in its place one far more grand and beautiful. But what still more surprised and grieved me was, the want of dignity and solemnity in the services themselves. There was a grand array of sacred vessels, to be sure, and the robes, both of the gods and the priests, were rich and imposing; but neither they who ministered, nor they who listened, behaved with that decorum to which I have always been accustomed. Some of the younger acolytes, especially, annoyed me by their levity, winking and whispering between prayers; and then the careless way in which they swung their censers and poured their libations; but above all, the shameful rapidity with which they chanted the hymns, mortified me beyond measure. I am amazed that the high priest tolerates such abuses. Truth to tell, however, these worthy men of Babylon seem to be in a hurry about everything; not merely their devotions, but all their business and pleasures are conducted in the same impulsive and tumultuous manner. How they dash along their streets, and rattle over their roads, and gobble down their viands, and jerk out their syllables, and ply their oars, and drive their slaves and their bargains; in a word, plunge through the work and play of the day with a swiftness and fury quite incomprehensible to us slow Assyrians. The very sands in their hour-glasses seem to chase each other faster than ours—the holy fires themselves to give a less clear and tranquil light. Such, at least, are the impressions made upon me, after an eight days' experience. Am I right, or not? You will call me over-nice, perhaps, and captious about trifles, to say nothing of repaying hospitality with ungracious criticism; and yet, my dear friend, do not these trifles make up the sum of our existence? Do they not shed far more light upon the character of a people, than all the sententious inscriptions of monoliths, the gaudy pageantry of palace-walls?

But not to dwell on this point, I was about to

add, that I was far more impressed with the services at the beautiful temple of Oannes. I could never weary of gazing at this charming pile, and the pleasant grove that surrounds it, its superb entablatures, the majestic figures that crown its battlements, and most admirable of all, the pictures that line its interior, and in which are embodied, with so much grace and feeling, the precious traditions of this worship. And, I repeat it, the ritual itself is far more simple and touching, and comes home more to the hearts and understandings of the multitude of the faithful than does that of the greater temple. The music, too, delighted me. I have never heard the "Hymn to the Sea" given with such pathos before. I confess it, O Telassar, there is no god in all our pantheon, before whose altars I throw myself more gladly, or pour out my vows more fervently. True, even in this service, there are figures and emblems that must forever remain mysteries and stumbling-blocks to the rude minds of the masses; rites, too, whose quaint simplicity may offend the fastidious, or provoke the sneers of scoffers; but to us, who apprehend aright the profound truths that underlie them, and the inestimable benefits to mankind which they symbolize, how reverend, how beautiful are they in our eyes! I marvel not, indeed, at the popularity of this worship, or at the progress which it is making all through Syria and Judea, and can only wish that it was a more prominent feature in our own faith, and that the image of its god was more conspicuous in our Assyrian temples.

But Belus bless me, is it so late? I must throw by my reed forthwith. I ought, this very moment, to be paying my respects, and delivering your message, to the illustrious Hatach; after which we are to have the honor of breaking bread in the house of the lord chamberlain.

* * * * * * * *

We were most agreeably entertained last evening—without ceremony, ourselves and Adar being the only guests. I need not tell you what a charming talker our host is, nor how much wisdom there is under his drollery. He had many pleasant anecdotes to tell us, about the king and royal family, all illustrating the amiableness as well as strength of his character, and his untiring vigilance for the welfare of his people.

I was by no means disappointed in our host's library and gallery of antiques, of which you have so often spoken to me. Indeed, I have never seen so many choice papyri and tablets in any private collection before; to say nothing of his superb cabinet of gems. But, since you were here, there has been one very remarkable addition to his art-treasures, namely, a complete series of tiles, illustrating the prominent events of Babylonian and Assyrian annals. There are two hundred in all, commencing with the apotheosis of Ninus, and ending with the coronation of Bel-Adon. They are by far the largest I have ever seen, being three cubits and a half in breadth, two and a half in height, and two inches in thickness. They are executed after the designs of the first artists of the Sacred College, and are surrounded by highly-ornamented borders—no two borders being alike—showing a surprising fertility of invention in the designers. They are numerically arranged on sliding frames—most ingeniously contrived—within a large and elegant case of box-wood, beautifully stained, and inlaid with ebony and ivory; the whole, when shut, being inclosed within a superbly-embroidered silk cover. I forget how many golden talents our host had to pay for this—if I may so call it—magnificent pictorial history of the empire. It is, indeed, a master-work—so admirable in drawing, so accurate in costume, so vivid in coloring. I have seen nothing, since leaving home, that I have so coveted. After long lingering over its beauties, and listening to the explanations of our host, we were regaled with some excellent music on the harp, by members of the royal band, and concluded a most agreeable evening with a delicious moonlight sail on the river.

We have been, this morning, to see a vessel, recently launched, and whose beauty is the talk of the town. We were amply repaid for our trouble. She leaves, in a day or two, for Nineveh, being, indeed, a present from his majesty to King Sennacherib. She is by no means remarkable for size, being quite overshadowed, in this respect, by scores of merchantmen and ships-of-war in the royal docks; but in symmetry of model, grace, fleetness, perfect obedience to her helm, strength, and finish—both of wooden and hanging gear—and the thorough discipline of her crew, it would be hard, I should think, to find her superior in any port on earth. The images on her prow and stern are the perfection of carving and coloring, and her huge, snow-white sail, with its golden devices, and its fringes and tassels of purple silk, is as gorgeous as a dream. What most struck my eye, however, were two exquisitely light and airy corridors, surrounding the upper cabins. I should have said, by the way, that it was a three-decker, of ten banks. These corridors are formed by small cedar pillars, highly polished, with elaborate capitals, supporting a series of semi-circular arches, the pillars and arches being alternately blue and white, and the capitals gilt; the whole producing a novel and, to me, beautiful effect. I will not undertake to describe the sumptuousness of the sleeping chambers, or the banqueting chambers, with their checkered floors, and brilliant carpets, and hangings, and daintily-carved couches; or the superb chime of bells, and the water-clock of the state cabin; or the exquisite miniature temple and altar, on the upper deck; still less, the thorough appointments of the kitchen and pantry. Enough to say, that all that is beautiful or ingenious, in bronze, or gold, or silver, or porcelain, is to be found in them. The vessel is truly a wonder, throughout, and as complete an embodiment as one would wish to show a stranger, of the power, splendor, and luxury of the empire. No such lovely burden did the Tigris ever bear on its waters, and its arrival at the metropolis will surely be greeted with acclamations.

Congratulate me, my dear friend, congratulate me. I have just returned from the palace, after a two hours' audience. His majesty has been pleased to prefer my designs to those of the other competitors. He seemed especially gratified with the eastern façade of the building, and with the laying out of the gardens. He complimented me warmly, also, on the drawings for the new bridge, but would have preferred more arches, and more statues crowning its balustrades. Though not quite convinced by his reasoning, I shall, of course, modify my plans accordingly. And so my mind is at rest, and my destiny decided for the coming twelvemonth, at least. Thank the gods! I shall eat my meal in peace to-night, and say my prayers with a grateful heart. Zethar, I am sure, will not be dissatisfied with this arrangement, and, I trust, will derive profit, as well as pleasure, from his residence here.

But no more to-day. I shall write you, at least, twice a month, my dear Telassar, and hope you will find time to reply to my letters. And so I commend you and your good household to the favor of the gods.

MEMUCAN.

LETTER III.

ZETHAR IN BABYLON TO HEGAI IN NINEVEH.

I HAVE not forgotten my promise, dear kinsman, to give you some account of our journey hither; and, as the best mode of so doing, I will make a few extracts from my diary.

Tenth day of second month of Season of Fruits of the thirteenth year of our Lord and King Sennacherib.

This afternoon, we bade farewell to our good friends upon the quay, and embarked on board the "Gazelle," bound for Babylon. We are anticipating a right pleasant voyage. Our vessel is small, but handsome, comfortable, and well-manned. We have the exclusive use of her, with the privilege of stopping wherever and as long as may suit our pleasure or convenience. Our only fellow-passenger is Mehuman, a colonel in the Fourth Legion, who has just obtained a three-months' leave of absence from his majesty, on the score of ill-health, and who accompanies us as far as his native city of Rehoboth. He is an old friend of father's, who invited him to join us, as the least fatiguing mode of getting home. Our captain, a Sidonian, seems to be a well-disposed, skillful fellow, with a wonderful power of lungs, which he at times perverts to profane uses. Our cabin is airy and cheerful, and our cook an artist.

What a lovely evening! We have just come to anchor beneath the fortress of Resen, having had a charming four-hours' sail. Never before did it appear to me so charming; but who shall presume to describe it, or to set forth the succession of beautiful pictures that Nineveh and its environs present to the traveler? Such combinations of groves, parks, gardens, pleasure-houses, villas, palaces, temples, towers, statues, obelisks; such felicitous groupings of objects, such vivid and various hues! Surely, no other jewel of earth hath such a setting as this. So thought I, at least this evening, as I stood gazing on its beauties illuminated as they were by the golden light of the departing sun, and reflected, with softened lustre, in the stately river. I lingered fondly over the picture, till the last ray had gilded the loftiest of its myriad towers, and then threw myself upon the deck, and poured out my thanks to the gods, who had cast my lot amid such scenes.

After a pleasant supper, the colonel and I had a

few games of draughts together, while father busied himself with his drawings.

11th. Very early this morning, my father and myself clambered up the hill, and, after seeing the sun rise, from the tower of Sardanapalus, took guides and torches, and explored some of the recently-excavated chambers of his palace. Imperfectly as we discerned their contents, father was quite as enthusiastic about them as he has been about the previous discoveries. One chamber especially delighted him, with its admirably-preserved series of slabs, illustrating a campaign of Sardanapalus in Syria. The colors seem as fresh as if laid on yesterday, and the figures are very spirited and lifelike. I confess, I could not see, though, that marvelous difference between them and the works of our own artists that father does. One would think, to hear him talk, that art, science, faith, all the good things of life, had sadly degenerated since those days. It may be so; but I am too young, and too little of a philosopher by nature, to appreciate his reasonings on these points. One curious stone, by the way, we stumbled over, which was discovered the day before our visit; its inscription being a brief history of the palace itself. It speaks of one built long before the time of Sardanapalus, by one of his forefathers, its having fallen into decay and ruin, and his restoration of it; reciting its plan, and the gold, and silver, and copper, and cedar, and ivory, and all the precious and far-brought materials expended upon it; concluding with an invocation of the blessings of the gods upon his labors. And *this*, forsooth, is the answer to his prayers! Three centuries have hardly elapsed, and lo, his own work is dug out of the earth in its turn, and in its ruined chambers to-day are artists exploring, scholars musing, clowns gaping, and moralizers prattling, as I do now! And future kings, of course, are to repeat the same vain labors here. Meanwhile, the excavations are going on with great promptness and system, and all the hidden treasures of the spot will soon be laid bare. Father would willingly have spent the day here; but we contented ourselves with a two-hours' visit, finding our fellow-voyager up when we returned, and by no means indisposed for breakfast.

We have been gliding quietly along all day, with a gentle breeze behind us; threading our way amongst a fleet of vessels of all sorts, from the vast rafts, groaning beneath their huge burdens of basalt and limestone, down to the gaily-daubed cockle-shells of the fishermen. We have passed many pleasant gardens and cheerful towns. The fields have given up their treasures, and the laborers are at work in the threshing-floors. This afternoon we have met several huge caravans, on both sides of the river. Conspicuous among them, I noticed that of our great merchant, Hamesh, with its mile-long train of camels—their gay palanquins and scarlet trappings making a bright picture as they passed, and their bells discoursing merry music.

12th. We have spent several pleasant, busy hours to-day at Arvan, at the magnificent armory. The colonel was not well enough to accompany us, but gave us a line of introduction to the commanding officer, who was very civil to us. It would take many days rightly to examine the details of this vast establishment, with its immense forges and founderies, its long lines of work-shops, its huge army of workmen, and to appreciate the order, and discipline, and admirable distribution of labor that prevail in it. Here the student of war may learn all the weapons of his calling, and the processes of making them, from the humblest spear or arrow-head, up to the most complicated and colossal engine. A graphic remark of the superintendent best illustrates the resources of the place. "Five hundred thousand men," said he, "might enter yonder portals without a weapon, and, in two little hours, sally forth a thoroughly appointed host." Such stores of arms are kept here in reserve, besides those continually sent away for the uses of the government! The gallery of engines impressed me deeply. What a collection of monsters, drawn up in grim array on both sides; catapults of all sizes, rams, porcupines, spiders, scorpions, chimeras, I know not how many dreadful devices; now silent and tenantless, but who knows how soon to be lined with warriors, or crammed with deadly missiles, and to be dashed, amidst shouts and execrations, against the walls, or to pour forth their terrible contents into the hearts of hostile cities. "Pretty playthings, are they not?" remarked the keeper of the gallery to me—a dry, sarcastic little man; "here's a darling for you, now," pointing to a hideous machine, which, at every discharge, he said, sent five tons of stones flying through the air. "We have already tried the virtues of this medicine," he added, on several rebellious towns in Judea and Samaria, and a very few doses have effectually quieted the patient." In the same sneering vein, he eulogized the performances of another frightful-looking invention, which he called the "Sleeping Beauty." From this hall of horrors, we issued forth into a vast court filled with chariots, several thousands in all, I should think; in every variety of pattern and finish, and gracefully grouped in a series of concentric circles, with eight avenues radiating from the centre. The effect was grand, as you stood in the midst, and looked round upon this goodly congregation, and mentally contrasted their quiet beauty and orderly array with the wild scenes of tumult and slaughter they are yet destined to figure in. From this court, we were shown through a series of superb halls, filled with armor, most conveniently and tastefully arranged—each hall being set apart for its own particular weapon, and were finally conducted to the Gallery of Gems, as it is called—a magnificent room, in which only the most costly products of the work-shops are deposited. Many of its treasures have been removed to the palace at Nineveh, many have been sent as gifts to friendly monarchs, or bestowed as rewards for distinguished service in the field; still there remains a superb collection—golden-crested helmets, with exquisitely wrought lappets, inimitably carved shields, with appropiate inscriptions, swords blazing with gems, daggers beautiful as dreams, bow-cases, with most dainty and fanciful devices, pictured banners, and standards of marvelous embroidery. The most conspicuous ornament of the room is a newly-finished triumphal car, which is to make its first appearance in public on occasion of the dedication of the new temple. The bas-reliefs on its panels are miracles of grace and beauty; too beautiful to be described in humble prose. But I can write no more this evening—my eyes ache, my brain is bewildered with the crowd of images that press upon it.

13th. Here we are at the charming town of Calah. Just before reaching the quay, a slight mishap befell our little craft—she having been run into by a wretched tub of a ferry-boat, and somewhat bruised about the prow, to say nothing of the loss of her graceful figure-head. Strong language prevailed, for a moment, on both vessels ; our good colonel, I grieve to add, quite forgetting his sickness, in the energy of his maledictions. This accident will detain us till to-morrow evening; but as we had determined to spend a day here, at any rate, it is no disappointment to us.

14th. Another pleasant day. Let me see ; we first called to pay our respects to his Excellency, Ophar, one of the judges of the city, and a friend of uncle Telassar's. After a brief visit and a promise to return to dinner, we sallied forth to explore the quarries, and then visited several of the sculptors' studios, where we saw many admirable works, both in limestone and alabaster. As I had never seen these —the largest and finest quarries in the empire—father was determined that we should not neglect the present opportunity. A pleasant ten-minutes' walk brought us to the principal entrance—one of Ophar's slaves, a lively, intelligent fellow, accompanying us as guide. I had, indeed, but a faint conception of the extent and riches of the place, or of the amount of labor daily expended in it. It is almost as large as the town itself, with its squares, streets, and avenues, and its thousands of workmen, captives, and malefactors from all lands. What a noisy, busy scene, to be sure ! Such a clicking of picks, and din of hammers, and grating of saws, and creaking of timbers, I never heard before. And then the struggles of the oxen, and the shouts of the drivers, and the cracking of the whips, and, over all, the fierce voices of the overseers, as, with curses and many blows with their spears, they urged on to their tasks the lazy or sullen laborers. What a set of wretches these last! Some inexpressibly sad, others brutally apathetic, others savage and malignant; their dark faces and dingy costume strikingly contrasting with the shining, beautiful material on which they were working. As we stood gazing at an enormous block, just cut, and I should think at least forty cubits in length, and then at the ponderous machinery for removing it to its sledge, suddenly the trumpets sounded, summoning the laborers to their noontide meal. Curious was it to see the simultaneous dropping of their tools, and their silent, rapid march to the prison hard by, leaving the place strangely still and vacant. We wandered about for some time here. Notwithstanding the immense masses that have been carried away, but little impression seems to have been made upon the resources of the quarries. Centuries of labor must elapse, indeed, before their treasures are exhausted—before the myriad thoughts, and images, and annals, that are now slumbering here, shall be duly embodied, and sent forth to take their places in the world's art and history. Meanwhile, what mighty events may not the gods have in store? What wars, what revolutions, what births and deaths of empires, what precious discoveries, on earth and in the heavens, may not these same stones be called on to illustrate and to recite! I was in the midst of some such fit of musing as this, when we found ourselves at the northern gate of the quarries, nearly a mile to the left of that by which we had entered, and through which we passed, on our way back to the town. Not far from this gate is the studio of Hathan, the most distinguished of the sculptors of Calah. We did not find him at home, but one of his students politely showed us through the apartments. Of the many interesting works here, both in limestone, and basalt, and alabaster, I was most struck with a pair of holy bulls, just finished, and designed for the temple of Nebo, at Opis. Though elaborated to the last degree, there is yet a grandeur and majesty about them which I have never seen equaled. A group of lions in yellow limestone, full of grace and spirit, and in every variety of attitude, also held my eyes captive for a long time. Father called my attention to two sublime figures—being the divinities of our two great rivers, and intended to ornament the eastern front of the arch at the entrance of the grand canal. He was also much interested in a series of slabs, designed for the same structure, and on which all the pompous ceremonial with which its corner-stone was laid is portrayed with great minuteness. There are some fine works, too, here, in black basalt, both statues and in relief; among them an admirable likeness of his majesty—a sitting figure. The expression and drapery are alike excellent; but I have no patience with the material itself, nor do I believe the gods intended it for such lofty uses. How it ever found favor with our artists, is to me a mystery, being so repulsive and unmanageable, so wearying to their strength, so hard upon their tools.

From Hathan's we went to the studio of Shobal, the famous worker in bronze. His rooms are few and small, as he mostly confines his labors to the miniature department of his art. Indeed, it is only through a strong magnifying glass that you can get an insight into the marvelous beauty and finish of his compositions. I have seen nothing like it at Nineveh, nor could I have conceived it possible that such a world of history and poetry could have been packed up within the compass of a square inch. But so it is, and when you bring the lens to bear upon it, every group, almost every figure and tree in the composition, is expressive and characteristic. One cup quite enchanted me; a little thing, about two inches and a half in diameter, by two in depth, and yet, within its magic circle, all the incidents of a lion-hunt were depicted with amazing spirit and fidelity; one-half representing the pursuit on the plains, with horses and chariots, the other, the more desperate and perilous chase among the mountains. The work is incised, and, of course, more elaborate and expensive than the same subject would be, if embossed. I forget how many hundred figures there are in all, or how many hundred shekels the artist values it at. I should have dearly loved to have bought it for my good Hegai; but, alas, such costly toys belong to the cabinets of kings, and not to the humble chamber of students. And surely the artist ought to be munificently rewarded for such works as these, when we consider the outlay of time and skill, and the risks involved—a single maladroit blow of the punch or graver often marring, beyond repair, the labor of months, or even years.

We next looked in, for a moment, at the Royal Foundry, where they were busy making preparations for the casting of a colossal statue of King Sargon. We are sorry that we cannot wait to see the process, which is to take place in a few days. They showed us, however, the designs, both for the statue, and the bas-reliefs on its pedestal; the former being by Hathan, and the others by his son. The treatment is strictly religious, the king being in full pontifical costume, with the mace in his left hand, and his right raised in the usual attitude of benediction. It is to be erected on a lofty platform, in the centre of the city, and will be nearly forescore cubits in height, including the pedestal. I quite agreed with father in his admiration of it, and can imagine the fine effect it would produce at sunset, outlined against the glowing sky, or, finer still, under the solemn moonlight.

On returning, we found our excellent host, who had long since got through the judicial duties of the day, and was quite impatient, indeed, for his dinner. The repast was a most satisfactory one. I don't know when I have dipped my hand in nicer dishes than those which his lovely daughter set before us. We did not see his wife, who is much of an invalid, nor his son, now on a visit at Babylon. Neither his grave functions, nor his advanced years, made themselves manifest in Ophar's manners or conversation. On the contrary, he was full of fun, and was wagging his silver beard continually, both at his own jokes, and those of an Ethiopian slave in attendance, even older than himself, and who was evidently a privileged jester in the family. Some of their pleasantries certainly bordered on the indecorous; leaving the impression, moreover, that our host, though, no doubt, very loyal and devout in externals, is a good deal of a free thinker at bottom. He has been occupying himself considerably of late, in building a tomb in his garden, which he insisted upon showing us, and about which he made many queer remarks. It is a handsome and substantial structure, somewhat in the Egyptian style, adorned with appropriate paintings and comfortable couches, and surrounded with nice walks, flower-beds, fish ponds, everything, indeed, as he expressed it, to make death snug and pleasant. His coffin had come home that very day. He was quite delighted with it, and asked us if we did not think that he had shown good taste in the selection? It certainly was a superb piece of alabaster, and the lid covered all over with exquisite carved work. To our dismay, he had it removed, and ordered the Ethiopian to get in, and, as he said, try the fit of it. The slave obeyed instantly, and when fairly on his back, grinned and rolled his eyes about, in the most absurd manner. Father, I thought, was a good deal shocked at this exhibition. He said nothing, however, merely remarking to me, after we had parted with our entertainer, that his excellency was a very eccentric person, and not to be construed too literally.

On our way to the quay, we overtook the Sidonian, who was urging forward, with many kicks and maledictions, a couple of our crew, who had been abusing their leisure, by getting drunk. We were glad to get back to our pleasant little cabin, where we found the colonel reposing very quietly, having apparently fallen asleep over a chapter of Zoroaster.

15th. Edar. We arrived here about mid-day, and have just returned from a visit to the governor of the town. He is a particular friend of Mehuman's, and, as the walk was but a short one, he insisted on accompanying us. We were kindly received by the governor, who is a tall, splendid-looking man, and, moreover, a great military enthusiast. The prominent topic, indeed, of his conversation, was the merits of a machine which he had just been perfecting, to wit, a scythe-armed chariot. After describing it at length, he took us down into the court-yard of the palace, where several of these grim objects were drawn up in one corner. It made one shudder to look at them, with their huge, glittering blades projecting on either side—some with two, others with four, and even six blades. I could not help noticing the blood-stains on some of them. "Ah, yes," said the governor, "it was but yesterday that we tried their capabilities on a hundred or two of rascally convicts, in an inclosed place, just outside of the walls; and I assure you, colonel, we had every reason to be satisfied with the result." He then went on to relate, in the most cold-blooded way, all the details of the experiment; the beautiful behavior of the horses, the skill of the charioteers, the admirable way in which the chariots turned and wheeled, the velocity with they were borne onward, and, above all, the clean work (as he phrased it) which they made with the malefactors; taking off heads, arms, and legs, cleaving in twain trunks, both of men and beasts, without a single overturn, or the loss of a single scythe. All this he recited with the same satisfied, self-complacent air, with which a barber might prattle of the performances of some favorite razor. I was greatly shocked, I confess. Not so our invalid colonel, who quite brightened up on the occasion, and entered into the subject with true professional zeal. He regretted that he could not have witnessed the experiment; he had long thought that this important weapon of war had been neglected, and was glad to see it revived and improved ; he predicted a brilliant career for it in future battle-fields, and only regretted that its operations were confined to service in the plains, for he would dearly love to give those accursed Armenian rebels a taste of its qualities ; spoke of it, in short, as a veteran campaigner might be expected to speak. Oh, the heartlessness, the atrocities of war ! Who would think, to hear these two men talk, that they were, as I know them to be, good husbands, kind fathers, loyal subjects, sincere worshipers ? Ah, dear, what a bundle of inconsistencies is human nature, what a frightful complication of mysteries, human life !

16th. Rehoboth. This is most justly called Rehoboth the Beautiful, with its picturesque fortress, its pleasant streets, its gay gardens, its famous wheat-fields, its superb girdle of olive-groves. Our fellow-traveler, it seems, had been expected for some time, as there was quite a retinue of servants waiting for him. He insisted on our riding with him to his house, some two miles from the landing-place. On our way thither, we overtook one of his sons, a handsome boy of some twelve years, with bright eyes and golden ringlets. He was driving a miniature chariot, drawn by four snow-white goats ; a very complete little turn-out, with glittering harness, each goat being also dressed out in rosettes and ribbons, with a string of little bells about its neck. He informed us that it was a birthday present from an old uncle. He had a pretty little sister in the chariot with him, and likewise his bow and quiver —he being on his way home from a small gathering of archers of his own age, who had been shooting for prizes, two of which he proceeded to show us, as the trophies of his skill.

It was pleasant to see the affectionate greetings that passed between father and children. Their mother, it seems, has been dead but a few months, nor had the household yet recovered their accustomed cheerfulness. There was another child at home, who interested me exceedingly; a little fellow hardly six years old, yet of rare intelligence. I found it impossible to puzzle him, either in arithmetic or geography. He can print on clay, too, and write on papyrus, almost as fast as I can, without missing a wedge, or misplacing a letter. He means to be a priest, he says; and truly, if he goes on accumulating knowledge as he has begun, he will be a bright light in the priesthood. Before going to bed, his father made him repeat a hymn to Ashur, which he did with marvelous propriety and feeling.

The colonel gave us an excellent supper, and, if the wines he placed before us were faithful representatives of his cellar, it must, indeed, be a paradise for the bibber. His library is rather small and miscellaneous, having been much neglected, he says, of late. He showed us some interesting drawings of battles in which he had taken part, and also the sword, shield, and helmet, with which he had begun life, he said, some forty years ago, and which had been presented him by good King Sargon himself. There was a manuscript, also, which he evidently took great pleasure in showing to us, and the contents of which he seemed to have by heart. It was a translation, into Assyrian verse, of sundry fragments of the famous old Greek singer, Homer, made about a century since, by an ancestor of our host, and himself a distinguished soldier in his day, while stationed at Sardis ; the originals having been copied by him at various times, as they fell from the lips of wandering minstrels. Since then, of course, Greek songs, both original and translated, have been heard in our market-places, and may be found in many of our libraries ; but, at that time, such a collection must have been a great curiosity. I am not scholar enough to judge of the fidelity of the rendering; but the lines themselves had a very pleasant flow, and were quite grand at times, presenting many vivid pictures and soul-stirring sentiments. The colonel recited several favorite passages, not with the same animation and effect as if he had been well, still, sufficiently so to help the evening along very agreeably.

17th. A quiet day we have had of it. We left our good host at a very early hour this morning, and have been on the wing ever since, only stopping a few moments at Arbo, to buy some milk and fruit. Father has been at work all day with his plans and calculations, as I intended to have been, over my astronomical tablets; but lo and behold! when I came to open the parcel, instead of my sky-studies for the coming month, I found that I had stumbled over a most dismal collection of law-forms, deeds, wills, marriage-articles, stupid contracts of all sorts. Can it be, that that rascally bibliopole at Rehoboth intended to impose on me thus? Or, in the hurry of the moment, did he hand me the wrong package? I would willingly give him the benefit of the latter supposition, but that I recall a certain villainous twinkle of the eye, that almost confirms the former. Confound the scoundrel! Such horribly fine print, too! It is bad enough to sacrifice one's eyes to sound science and authentic history; but to throw them away upon such interminably verbose and dreary trash as this! Out upon it! In my fury I consigned the documents to the Tigris. Belus help the fish that swallows them!

18th. We reached Dura just before sunrise, after sailing all night. It has been a grand holiday here, being the governor's birthday. We have spent our time mostly with our young kinsman, Meran, who has just completed his second year at the military academy here. He is a fine, handsome fellow, and seemed right glad to see us. He quite distinguished himself in the military exercises, which formed the principal entertainment of the day, and which were duly graced with the governor's presence. Meran found a capital station for us, from which to view the show. First came a review of the troops by his excellency; some two thousand students in all, in every variety of armor and equipment—horsemen and chariots, heavy and light-armed infantry, archers and slingers. I was charmed with the grace and precision of their movements, and with the superb music of the band. Then we had a foot-race, in which a hundred beautiful youths took part; a horse, a shield, and a golden chaplet being the prizes of the three victors. Then came some admirable specimens of archery; but, above all, did a corps of youthful slingers distinguish themselves, by the marvelous rapidity and skill of their performances. A large grotesque figure of wet clay was set up at a distance of a hundred yards, and in an incredibly short space of time it was covered all over with oval-pointed bullets; at least nineteen-twentieths of those discharged having lodged in it. Pebbles, it seems, are quite out of use in the army, and are only fit, said M., to pepper birds with. I had no conception of the effectiveness of this weapon; but my eyes were opened on seeing the impression made upon this image. Loud plaudits greeted the efforts of the young marksmen. The exercises closed with the assault and capture of a miniature fortress, erected in the midst of the capacious and beautiful grounds attached to the academy. The siege lasted about an hour, and was thoroughly and effectively rendered, from the first summons of the trumpet, to the carrying off of the spoils. Sham-fights generally are things to yawn over; but the spirit and fidelity of this performance quite riveted us to our seats; and yet no blood was spilt, and only one ankle sprained, during the whole representation. After the fall of the fortress, came an onslaught of a very different nature, in the shape of a banquet, in the great hall of the academy, and in which both besiegers and besieged enacted prodigies of valor. So it seemed to us, as we surveyed the field from one of the galleries overlooking the hall. In the afternoon, Meran came down to see us, and remained aboard till sunset. He would have staid longer, but he had to make his arrangements for the procession this evening; the students all marching by torch-light to pay their vows at the temple of Merodach. Father retired early, while I amused myself by wandering about the streets, watching the motley groups gathered around the jugglers and the dancing girls, or listening to the doleful ditties of the ballad-singers. In the palace-square, which was finely illuminated, there was a grand roasting of sheep and oxen, and a distribution of wine and loaves to the people. It was long after midnight before the town was quiet.

19th. We were detained some time this morning by the non-appearance of several of our mariners, who had been participating quite too freely in yesterday's festivities. The sun was full four hours high, before the last of the delinquents was kicked aboard.

We are fairly in the low countries at last; not the faintest vestige of a hill to be seen. A few hours' sail brought us abreast of the entrance of the eastern canal—the first of that series of magnificent works whose praises father has been singing all day. And truly, the most thoughtless traveler could not look upon them, for the first time, without emotion, bearing, as they do, the precious waters of the Tigris —the very life-blood of the land—to so many myriads of fields and gardens, giving existence and support to so many thriving towns and smiling villages; in a word, turning these vast plains, else a parched and barren wilderness, into a scene of beauty and fruitfulness, unparalleled on earth. The history of these works, the grand conceptions of their designers, the science, labor, and treasure expended upon them, these are topics on which father is always ready to talk. He gave me many interesting details as to the mode of their construction, the cost of repairs, the scale of tolls and of prices paid by the consumers, and the many contrivances for preventing the abuse or waste of the waters. After reading the grand inscription on the face of the tower erected here in their honor, we climbed to the top, and looked down on a most superb picture, its crowning ornament being these canals and their tributaries, with their shining lines intersecting it in all directions, like a vast network of silver spread over the land, and of all dimensions, from the spacious channels dotted with boats and barges, down to the tiny threads, glistening along the borders of the humblest gardens. After spending a couple of hours here, we reëmbarked, and arrived at Samara about an hour before sunset. We immediately reported ourselves to the officer on the quay—this being the last town before entering Babylonia. He was very prompt and courteous in his examination, and in less than ten minutes we were under way again.

Shortly after leaving Samara, we came in sight of the wall of Ninus, stretching off grandly to the southwest, pierced here and there by stately archways, its lofty battlements and long line of receding towers bathed in the mellow light of sunset, while ever and anon the parting rays would be caught and reflected from the glittering armor of some distant sentinel. A grand picture; far different, indeed, from that we had gazed on in the morning, but, in its way, equally fine and suggestive. It was after dark when we reached the fortress at the water's edge, in which the wall terminates. Our trumpet was promptly responded to from the shore, and, after laying to for a few moments, we were duly boarded by a centurion, followed by a couple of lantern-bearing attendants. He was a very surly, silent person, not vouchsafing to throw even a word at us; but, after a grim survey of our passports, and of the license of the Sidonian, he gave forth one solitary grunt of assent, and we were permitted to proceed.

20th. It was late in the night when we passed

Opis. I got up, and had a glimpse of the beautiful city, slumbering in the moonlight, and of the temple of Nebo, rising majestically out of its midst—the glow of its sacred fires bringing out into strong relief the stately obelisks in front of it, and the divine images that crown its summit. We had intended to spend some days here; but concluded, on the whole, to postpone our visit till our return from Babylon.

Our voyage to-day has been very pleasant. True, the scenery is somewhat monotonous, and the river has lost its clearness; but then the indications of plenty and prosperity that everywhere greet the eye, are most cheering to behold. This season, especially, the toils of the husbandman have been most bounteously rewarded. The barns are bursting with their treasures—the granaries fairly groaning beneath the spoils. Such prolific kitchen gardens, too! I never knew, till to-day, what cucumbers were, or melons. Everybody looks smiling and contented. Good cheer is inscribed in unmistakable characters on every man and beast that you meet. What groups of chubby children have we seen playing about the doors, or in the fields!—what comfortable-looking cattle!—what plump poultry! And oh, the date-groves! Never did I behold such golden clusters before, both hanging beneath their broad leaves and gathered in great yellow heaps on the ground.

21st. Accad. Last night, for the first time since leaving home, have the musquitoes really annoyed us; this morning, too, I confess, the fervor of my devotions has been impaired by the continued assaults of these malevolent and most intrepid little persecutors. Typho take them! say I. How any mortal can find music in their songs, or comfort in their caresses, is to me a mystery. And yet the men of Egypt, we are told, worship them, build altars to them, and offer oblations, and put up petitions. Why is this? Do they seek thus to propitiate the Evil One, from whom they spring, or do they indeed recognize in them hidden virtues—blessings in disguise? What possible attribute of a good God these creatures can symbolize, I have not faith or insight enough to discover. Father slaughters them without remarks, and would, no doubt, consider all such speculations very unprofitable.

We, of course, have been to see the boast of Accad—the tomb of Thunderbolt, the illustrious and dearly beloved steed of the divine Semiramis, whose fleetness, strength, and beauty are the time-honored theme of the Assyrian minstrel. It certainly is a most interesting old monument, and we lingered long over its quaint inscription, and studied out the curious and elaborate sculptures with which it is enriched. It was restored and re-colored not long since, with great care, and the letters of the inscription deepened and refilled with copper.

22nd. We have reached Calneh—brisk, bustling, noisy Calneh—with its fleet of vessels, its thronged market places, and crowded caravansaries. What a hubbub! What a clatter of drays and shouting of sailors! I took a short walk in the street facing the quay, this morning, and was glad to get back. Such a stench and racket I have not encountered for a long time; so many beggars and thieves, too, and sinister-looking faces, young and old; such a multitude of wine and beer-shops, and of idle vagabonds hanging about them, singing filthy songs, or roaring at the jests of some vile story-teller. Afterwards I explored some of the pleasanter parts of the town, with father, on our way to the old temple of Nebo, one of the oldest buildings in the empire. It is a very small, plain structure, of no interest save to the antiquary, and forms a most striking contrast to the cumbrous magnificence of its modern namesake hard by. There is far more in Calneh to interest the merchant than the artist or student. It owes its importance, of course, entirely to its position directly opposite the entrance of the Grand Canal—that magnificent monument of Assyrian enterprise. I was amazed at the vastness of the basin, and at the multitude of vessels of all sorts, coming and going in almost unbroken succession. The arch that spans the entrance is rapidly approaching completion, more than a thousand laborers being at work at it continually. When finished, it will reach the great height of one hundred and fifty cubits, being in width one hundred, and in depth sixty, and will undoubtedly be the most grand and beautiful thing of its kind on earth; at least, if all the sculptures that are to decorate it are like those we saw at Calah. Our little Gazelle took her place demurely enough in the great procession, and was borne along, behind three stout mules, at the snail's pace of three miles an hour—very different from her usual sprightly movements. Only once, during the passage, did the animals break into a trot for about a minute. Our captain gave vent to his impatience in occasional execrations; but, for myself, I found the transit anything but tedious, what with my admiration of the canal itself, the busy, cheerful scenes through which we passed, and the infinite variety of vessels, travelers, and merchandise that we were meeting continually.

23rd. It was quite late at night, and a beautiful moonlight, when we came out into the Euphrates after an eight-hours' passage. Our little vessel seemed glad to spread her wings again, and to feel once more the throbbing of her oars, and danced along right merrily. This morning, when I awoke, the lofty walls and myriad towers of the great city were visible in the distance, while around us were all the evidences of our approach to a metropolis. Such a swarm of boats in the river; such a crowd of caravans, and wagons, and horsemen, and footmen, on the roads; such a complication of canals and bridges in all directions, and all seemingly alive with travelers. I was much struck with a stately procession of elephants, in gaudy trappings, that passed close by us, on the east side of the river, and on their way, we were told, to the royal park at Nineveh. They certainly moved in a very majestic manner, and as if fully conscious of the distinguished quarters to which they were destined. We passed several huge glass factories with their lofty chimneys, their black volumes of smoke tinged by the morning beams; vast brick-fields and lumber-yards, and dépôts innumerable. But the scene on the river most interested me. Such a crowd and variety of vessels, from the gay little fruit and flower boats, up to the magnificent three-deckers; from the black, little, kettle-shaped craft of the fishermen up to the enormous rafts, buoyed up by their thousands of sheep-skins, and bearing on their vast surfaces, houses and families, and cattle, and sheep, and bales, and bags, and boxes, without number. It was almost noon before we could extricate ourselves from this dense throng, and reach the eastern water-gate. After a few moments' detention and examination, we again took wing. Another half-hour's sail, and a most charming one, through a scene whose beauty and splendor can be surpassed only by those of one other city on earth, brought us to the palace-bridge, on the northern side of which we disembarked, and in a few moments more found ourselves beneath the hospitable roof of dear Adar, who gave us a right hearty welcome. Farewell, Hegai. May the gods preserve you.

ZETHAR.

* * * * * * *

Father's mission, you will be pleased to learn, is a successful one, and we may consider ourselves Babylonians for the present. He has written several letters to friends at home, which this will accompany. Have the kindness to forgive whatever you may find in it of tedious, or flippant, or extravagant, and believe the writer your constant and loving friend, ZETHAR.

LETTER IV.

TELASSAR TO MEMUCAN.

We were right glad, my dear Memucan, to receive your last pleasant letter, and to hear the good news contained in it. I was fully prepared for such a result, and, though sorry to be deprived of your agreeable company, I feel that you are at last fairly on the road to that success which your talents so richly deserve. Before I add another word, let me thank you most heartily, in the name of Zeresh, for that magnificent carpet you sent her. Its brilliant hues and beautiful design have created quite a buzz of admiration among our neighbors.

I have not much news to tell you, to-day. We have abundant rumors from the seat of war; but few authentic dispatches. The last, received yesterday, informs us that the two armies were within four days' march of each other. So we shall soon hear, of course, of sharp, and I trust, decisive fighting.

Among the newly-arrived visitors at the metropolis is Clœlius, the Roman ambassador, with gifts and missives from the good king Numa. I have had the honor of several interviews with him, both at the palace, and at my own house. Notwithstanding his imperfect knowledge of our language, I have derived both pleasure and instruction from his conversation. He is a man of noble presence, with an earnest, truthful countenance (over which occasionally flits a shade of sternness), and a tall, commanding figure. His dress is of exceeding simplicity—a white gown, of few folds, unornamented save by a narrow purple border. This, and his closely-trimmed hair and beard, form a striking contrast, certainly, to the flowing locks, and pictured robes, and abundant jewels of our own countrymen. He was my guest at supper, last evening, and we had much pleasant chat over our wine. I was pleased, by the way, to notice his evident fondness for children, and the good-natured way in which he submitted to the scrutinizing glances and manifold impertinences of little Zeresh. Among other things, he had many interesting particulars to tell about his royal master, his striking traits of character, and the romantic circumstances under which he ascended the throne. Numa, it seems, though a good soldier, is not by inclination a warrior. On the contrary, during the twenty years that he has reigned, he has done all he could to curb the martial spirit of his people, to encourage the arts of peace, and to give the ploughshare as honorable a place in their hearts as the sword. A poet and philosopher, he is, moreover, a religious reformer, and has made important innovations in the popular faith and ceremonial. Hard and perilous experiments these, truly, for any ruler to make; and yet, it would appear that no monarch was ever more beloved and revered. Not a sword in our little realm, said Clœlius, but would leap from its scabbard to avenge the first look of contumacy or rebellion that might be given him. He described him as a man of singular gentleness of aspect, and grace and dignity of manner. The gods have not blessed him with sons; but he has a lovely daughter the idol of Rome. He lives in a small, plain house, on one of the many little hills in the midst of which the town is built (the Palatine, I think he called it), and often goes about the streets in the simplest attire, and with no retinue whatever. I need not tell you, how strangely this sounded to an Assyrian ear. Clœlius went on to contrast, and in quite a piquant manner, his infant Rome, as he called her (and she has hardly seen more than fifty birthdays), her rude walls, scattered dwellings, and the plain fare and frugal habits of her people, with the pomp, luxury, and magnificence of our own Nineveh. It was really quite graphic and animated; and none the less so, for his pausing at times, and knitting his brows, while vainly seeking the needful words in which to clothe his ideas. Of these last he has an abundance, and is by nature an orator. "And yet, who knows," he added, "in how few centuries the picture may be reversed?" (I certainly could not help smiling at so romantic a suggestion.) "One thing is certain," he continued, "that our good Numa is fully possessed with the idea of the future greatness and glory of his kingdom. It is his thought by day, his dream by night. He is haunted continually with visions of it. Special messengers from the gods have unfolded the scroll of destiny before his wondering eyes. He is dazzled, overwhelmed by the grandeur of the revelation; saddened, too, at the thought, averse as he is to war and conquest, that the sword is to be the principal agent in bringing about this great consummation. These prophetic visions oppress his mind—color his whole existence. Therefore is it that he is, even now, sending forth his citizens to all nations, that they may explore them, study their laws, and arts, and customs; and that friendly relations may be established, if possible, with their monarchs." (It would hardly do to report this part of Clœlius's conversation to his majesty; though a derisive smile would probably be his only reply to it.) Our guest went on to speak of other points of difference between the two countries, dwelling, at some length, on the greater liberty given, and respect paid to women, by the Romans. "Nay," said he, "we even intrust the keeping of the sacred fires themselves to a select body of virgins, chosen by the monarch." (Strange, indeed, this last!)

I, in turn, had a good deal to say, in answer to the many questions of Clœlius, concerning our climate, and crops, and customs, and public works, and, especially, concerning our religion. "Do tell me," said he, "the meaning of all these holy images and emblems that everywhere meet the eye of the stranger; these sacred trees, and flowers, and fruits; these winged men and beasts; these majestic combinations of animals, that guard the portals of your temples and palaces, and the very gates of your cities; that adorn all your halls and galleries; that are embroidered on your garments, and carved on your couches and vessels, nay, on the very weapons that you wear. Above all, interpret for me that group which, you say, typifies your great national divinity."

He seemed pleased, I thought, with my explanation of this divine emblem; of the circle, denoting eternity, the wings, that speak alike of love and omnipresence, and of the majestic figure within, the embodiment of strength and wisdom; now in the act of launching the arrow of a righteous wrath against the impious unbeliever; now with hand extended as in benediction of the true worshiper. And so with all the other precious symbols of our faith, whose meaning I duly unfolded to him.

After a pause, Clœlius remarked, that the Roman was certainly a naked and unadorned religion, compared with the Assyrian; and yet that, after all, there were far more points of resemblance between them, than of difference. They had the same twelve great divinities; the same Father of all, to whom they bowed, as well as mortals; the same mysterious and holy fire, nourisher and sustainer of all things; the same deification of the heavenly host, and of the phenomena of nature; the same worshiping of divine attributes embodied, either actually or as imagined by men, in the multitude of created objects around them.

"True," I replied, "this, indeed, seems to be the only difference between us, that, from the greater liveliness of fancy, and quickness of perception, of us men of the East, there has sprung a corresponding enlargement of our pantheon, and a far more brilliant and, if you will, cumbrous ceremonial."

It seems that the good Numa is no friend to image-worship, and hath, indeed, sought to reduce, rather than multiply, the idols of the national religion. Clœlius, too, though somewhat fearful as to the result, yet appears to advocate the propriety of the innovation. I confess I could not see the force of his arguments. On the contrary, I am for increasing, as far as possible, the images of our faith, and the splendors of their worship. A religion without its carved and painted figures, its purple and fine linen, its gold and silver vessels, its incense and oblations, is, to me, the veriest mockery of a religion. What sophistry, too, to attempt to draw a distinction between those images that are merely painted on the mind's eye, or embodied in words, and the works of the carver or colorist! In either case, the enlightened mind looks beneath the image, at the hidden truth; but the multitude, who cannot discover truth, who know not language, who have no power to paint these mental images, are they, then, to be defrauded of the first great want of their hearts? Are they to have no household gods before whom to pour out their hopes, and fears, and vows; no sublime images in their temples, to which their poor, wavering eyes may turn for comfort, in which their weak, fluttering thoughts may find repose? I say again, I am for adding to, not taking from, the holy emblems of our religion, and would far sooner join with them, as do the men of Egypt, the worship of the cat, and the crocodile, and the onion itself (and may not some precious truths be embodied in its marvelous conformation?), than I would contract, by the veriest hair-breadth, the circle of our faith, or deduct one jot or tittle from the pomp of our ceremonial.

But I must not task your patience by any further report of our conversation. It was quite late at night when we parted company, at the door of my friend's house.

Since writing the above, I have had a delightful ramble with Clœlius, in the royal park. It was pleasant to watch his enthusiasm and evident astonishment at its vastness and magnificence. I hardly know which struck him most, the hunting-grounds, with their lofty walls, and artificial mountains, and forests, and water-courses — which, indeed, I could hardly persuade him were not the actual face of nature, but the creations of human toil and skill—or the gardens themselves, with their infinite variety of bird and beast, tree, fruit, and flower. We did not stay long in the former, as Clœlius expects to see a grand lion-hunt in a few days, having received an invitation from his majesty to take part in it; but the gardens detained us many pleasant hours. It was a holiday, and the good people were availing themselves freely of their accustomed privilege: thousands of men, women, and children were scattered about the grounds, and amusing themselves, as usual—petting the swans, feeding the gold-fish, sailing their little boats in the lakes, listening to the singing-birds and the fountains, and watching the ways of the animals. There was the usual crowd of youngsters about the huge cage of the monkeys; both performers and spectators laughing and chattering in high glee, while the cakes and nuts circulated freely. The cunning little beasts, how soon they find out, and how much they seem to relish, these same holidays! I was sorry, by-the-way, to see some additions to the collection of ourang-outangs. Out upon them, monsters—tailless, sightless, loathsome, obscene wretches—perpetual satires on humanity; why, why have the good gods embraced such creatures as these in the plan of their works? I noticed some ferocious apes, too, from India, that were strangers to me; nor, indeed, have I any wish to cultivate their acquaintance; huge things, as large as men; and in fact, it took two men to hold them, with chains around their bodies, at that. Of course, I did not fail to show our friend our famous lion, pride of Nineveh. You will be glad to hear that he is still in fine condition. Though the father of ten successive generations, his eye has lost none of its lustre, or his voice of its majestic music. Splendid creature, how we shall miss him when he dies, and what a superb monument and epitaph will set forth his praises to posterity! That poor bear, on the other hand, to whom Zethar was so fond of carrying gingerbread, seems to be in wretched health and spirits. He has lost both teeth and temper, since I last saw him. Oh that he could fairly jump out of that thick coat of his, so unsuited to our climate; or, at least, that he might have one more good roll in it, among the snows of his native Caucasus! But no, it is not so written on the tablets of destiny. The elephant, too, that other pet of our town, and perpetual theme of the talk of the small boys thereof, is, I grieve to say, in a declining state. He received with the utmost indifference the refreshments offered him, and executed his dance, at the keeper's bidding, with evident reluctance. It was a tame, spiritless affair, nor did he cut a single one of those pigeon-wings, so famous in former years. Poor Zophar, his dancing days are indeed over—his mission nearly ended. It was a relief to turn from his lame performance, and watch the sprightly movements of some gazelles, whose beauty, grace, and marvelous leaps quite delighted Clœlius. The birds, too, appeared to interest him greatly; the wind-swift ostriches, the stately swans, the flamingoes, with their black wings and snow-white bodies, and not least, the brilliant colors of the poultry, so different, he said, from the sober hues of the cocks and hens of Italy. The pheasantry was a great surprise to him; and, indeed, I know not when I have seen a more beautiful sight. After passing those large oval flower-beds, with their fanciful borders of box and laurel, which you admire so much, we crossed the circular grove, till we reached the edge of the central grass-plat. After waiting here a moment or two in the shade, the game-keeper came forth from his little lodge hard by, and with his whistle summoned the birds to their repast. Straightway a cloud of brilliant creatures, I know not how many thousands, came fluttering down from the trees all around us, in their robes of gold, and silver, and scarlet, and crimson, and purple, every imaginable variety of hue; a superb company, truly. They were not long in addressing themselves to the crumbs so punctually spread for them on their pleasant carpet of green. It was very amusing to watch their ways and manners — the silent assiduity with which some plied their bills, the chatterings and collisions of others over some contested morsel, and the airs and graces with which some of the more gorgeously attired ones strutted about, as if conscious of the presence of admiring beholders. We left them in the midst of their meal, our eyes fairly dazzled by the brilliancy of the scene.

Ah, the riches, the amenities of these gardens Can there be any other on earth, so beautiful, so sumptuous? What a privilege to dwell in a city that hath such appendages! What a place for the student of nature to learn his lessons in, and the philosopher to moralize, and the poet to weave his apologues! The children, too, what an inexhaustible source of amusement and instruction do they find here, and will, I trust, for countless generations! You have, of course, ere this, explored the beauties of those of Babylon, but how inferior they are to our own, in extent and richness!

This morning, I stole an hour from my duties, to show our friend some of the treasures of our Record-chamber, and to-morrow we purpose exploring together the magnificent Gallery of Antiquities. He sups to-night with the Archimagus, where I am also invited. In a few days he will leave for Ecbatana, that being the most eastern point of his journey. I hope, on his return, that he may be persuaded to visit Babylon, in which case I commend him to your loving regard. You will find him, I am sure, one of the noblest, most interesting men you ever conversed with.

I am sorry to inform you that our eccentric, absent-minded, archæological friend, Ethan, is in trouble; having been run down a few days since, by a baker's cart, while turning a corner, and badly bruised. Luckily, no bones were broken, though his cheek was laid open, and a most uncomely scar, I fear, will be the result. I called to see him a few moments yesterday, and found him doing well. It seems that the varlet who drove the cart, though most severely caned by a friend who witnessed the occurrence, was but little to blame; Ethan's eyes, at the time, though nominally open, having been virtually closed for all practical purposes. I could not resist asking him in what clime and era he was wandering, when the accident happened. You know he is generally about five centuries ahead of or behind the age. Puckering up his mouth in his usual queer way, he replied that he could not positively define his position, but, to the best of his recollection, he thought that he must have been inflecting the Hebrew verb, *Shagal*, at the moment of the collision. You are aware that he returned from Jerusalem, not long since, and has brought home with him a great admiration for the Hebrew language and writings. He is very enthusiastic, also, about their music.

"Maltreat and despise them as we may," said he, "between ourselves, they are a far more intellectual and accomplished nation than the Assyrians." He has lately been translating several of their songs and hymns; most of them, he says, composed by a famous singer, one David, who flourished between three and four centuries ago. He began life, it seems, a shepherd lad, then turned wandering minstrel, and finally, after many strange adventures, ended his days on the throne of Judea. Some of these compositions Ethan has heard chanted by the priests, and with a blended sweetness and power, he says, that completely carried him away. He insisted on my taking some of his translations home with me. I looked over a few of them last night; and with mingled feelings of indignation and admiration. Notwithstanding the intense egotism that pervades them, the bitter and contemptuous terms in which the writer speaks of all other faiths, and the grossly familiar way in which he addresses the only God, forsooth, that he deigns to recognize, there is still a glow of language, at times a fervor of devotion, and a power of describing natural scenes and objects, that are truly captivating, and force their way to the heart, in spite of all enmities and prejudices.

But I must bring this rambling, unsatisfactory letter to a close. I hope my next will be more interesting. I have not neglected your instructions concerning the drawings. They will positively go by to-morrow's caravan. Hegai has been reading to me some passages from Zethar's last letter to him, which he intends answering shortly. Embrace the dear youth for me, and likewise the excellent Adar.

TELASSAR.

LETTER V.

TELASSAR TO MEMUCAN.

'To the Most High and Mighty Sennacherib, King of kings and Lord of lords, humbly sendeth greeting his loyal servant Rabsaris: My last report left us newly encamped on the plains of Argish, after forcing the pass of Madiah, and dislodging the rebels from the hill-forts at either entrance. It is now my duty to announce the assault and capture of the town and fortress of Argish, after two days' fighting, and severe losses on both sides. The town itself, though well-manned, and bravely defended, could not long resist the skill and courage of our troops; but the taking of the citadel cost us many hours of hard labor, and many valiant soldiers—it being, as is well known to our Lord and King, one of the strongest and best-appointed fortresses in the empire, and utterly without approach, save on the western side. It was not till after twelve assaults, and in the face of incessant showers of stones, and darts, and firebrands, and boiling water, that we firmly planted, at last, our mounts against the walls, and brought our rams, and catapults, and scaling-ladders, into vigorous action. This once done, two hours' brisk work decided the fate of the place, and, as I write, the sacred banner of Assyria is floating from its topmost tower. Among the wretches who so desperately defended this stronghold, were, I grieve to add, the deserters from the Fifth Legion. The heads of these traitors, five hundred in number, I herewith send to our Lord and King. Their bodies I have fastened to stakes, and they are now hanging, in grim array, over against the walls of the captured city. Our loss, including some most worthy officers, will be found, as duly set forth in Roll Number three, appended to this report; and in Number four, that of the rebels, with the amount of captives, and cattle, and other spoil, as certified by the scribes.

"About the sixth hour after the fall of the fortress, and while preparing this dispatch, there came missives from Armavir, from King Milidduris, and with them his son, the young prince Minuas, bearer of the accompanying letter, which I have duly read, and herewith submit to our sovereign Lord. The prince, whom I shall straightway dispatch to Nineveh, will more fully explain its meaning. Meanwhile, I shall abstain from further hostilities, till our Lord and King's good pleasure is made known.

"All of which is laid at the feet of our Sovereign Lord by his faithful slave,

"RABSARIS.

"Signed and sealed, at Madiah, this thirteenth day of Third month of the Season of Fruits, and of the year of our Lord and King Sennacherib, the Thirteenth."

The above, my dear friend, is a copy of a dispatch received yesterday from our commander, and by me duly recorded, together with the letter of King Milidduris, to which it refers. In that letter, the rebel king, in the most penitential, abject mood, throws himself at the feet of His Majesty, beseeching forgiveness for the past, and full of promises for the future. He binds himself to pay, forthwith, all arrears of tribute, all the cost of the expedition against him, and furthermore the sum of two hundred talents of gold, and eight hundred talents of silver, into the royal treasury; and humbly sends his beloved son, Minuas, to be kept as a pledge for the performance of these conditions. These are the only important clauses in an epistle overflowing with epithets and protestations. I saw the young prince at the palace, this morning; a beautiful and intelligent youth, with an ingenuous countenance, and a voice of singular sweetness. I could see that His Majesty, notwithstanding his fierce and peremptory language, felt compassion for him, and was pleased with the firmness and dignity of his replies. He was dismissed, after a half-hour's audience, when the king dictated the following characteristic epistle :

"Sennacherib, King of Assyria, subduer of all lands, from the rising of the sun to the going down thereof, to Milidduris, King of Armenia : Thy letter and thy hostage are received. I accept thy conditions. Send thou thy messengers straightway hither with thy gifts and tributes, and account forthwith unto my servant Rabsaris, to the uttermost dram. Then may thy son depart in peace. Otherwise thou shalt not see his face more. For the last time, I pardon thy manifold transgressions, and give thee leave to rebuild thy towns, and retill thy fields. But if thou again, in word, look, or thought, rebellest, I spare thee no more, but will burn thy cities, lay waste thy palaces, and put thy people to the sword, yea, blot out thee and thy race from the memory of man forever."

This letter was immediately dispatched, with another, to our good general, who will, no doubt, soon close this business, and be with us again, ere many days. Last night, I read a long epistle of his to our friend Zothar, written a few days before the capture of Argish, in which he gives some details of the campaign, and speaks, with ill-suppressed exultation, of the prowess of his son Meres. There was, likewise, a postscript from the lad himself, which amused me greatly; in which he tells Hegai how beautiful it was to watch the flight of the death-dealing arrows, and the play and flash of the fatal swords, etc.; throwing about the epithets and metaphors with true boyish prodigality. Ah, dear, how we drop our adjectives as we grow older!

With the dispatch, came, also, the heads of the wretched deserters, mentioned by Rabsaris. A pyramid was soon built of them, in the market-place, where they were exposed all day, amid the jeers and execrations of the rabble, and, at night, were borne on spears, by torch-light, in dismal procession, to the gate of the eastern citadel, and tossed into the trenches, to become meat for vultures. So perish all traitors!

But enough of war news; and, indeed, this has created far less stir and talk in the city than it would have done under other circumstances, the thoughts of the people being quite engrossed with the preparations for the coming celebration—day after to-morrow, as you are aware, being set apart by his majesty for the dedication of our magnificent temple of the sun.

* * * * * * * *

I thought best to keep back my letter, in order to give you some account of our great holiday. I heartily wish you could have been present; for I am sure no such pageant was ever before seen within the walls of Nineveh. I will not pretend to give you all the details of its magnificence, but will glance at some of the more interesting features of the scene. And, first, the spectacle at sunrise. On the eastern front of the vast platform that encompasses the palace and the temple, and midway between the two, had been erected, on the day previous, a semicircular structure of wood, facing the east; spacious, though not lofty, its rows of seats being fitly carpeted and cushioned, and the whole exterior hung with tasteful drapery. In the centre of the space inclosed by it, stood our newly-finished obelisk—an honor, truly, to its builder—tallest, most stately, and exquisitely-carved stone on earth. Between the obelisk and the royal balcony was placed the fire-altar, while the altars of sacrifice occupied the space between the two extremities of the semicircle. Here were assembled, in silent adoration, all the chosen ones of Nineveh—the king and the royal family, the officers and servants of the royal household, the commanders of the different legions, the ambassadors and strangers of distinction, the royal astrologers and scribes, the members of the Sacred College, the priests of the different temples, the band of royal trumpeters and harpists, and a chosen choir of singers, youths and maidens—in all, several thousands—fitly grouped, and hushed in expectation of the coming god. Beautiful was the mute pomp—the solemn stillness of the scene. And now the first beam of day was seen to play upon the golden ball that crowns the summit of the obelisk. Forth, from the trumpets, came a long, loud, stirring note, and, as its echoes melted away in the distance, all, with one accord, threw themselves upon their faces, and addressed their souls to prayer. Then, slowly, and with the same silence, the king, and priests, and nobles—all the assembled congregation—rose to their feet; and now the venerable archimagus, with his attendant priests, descended the steps by the side of the royal balcony, and, advancing, knelt before the fire-altar, and began his solemn invocation to the god of day. Feeble as was his voice, and faltering his accents, yet so profound was the silence, that I hardly lost a word of his simple, touching petition. After the prayer, there was a moment's pause, and then the harps began to play a gentle prelude, gradually increasing in volume, and the choir, of a thousand singers, chanted the following hymn; the youths and maidens singing alternate stanzas, and all voices uniting in the last:

Again the monarch of the skies
  His glorious race hath run;
Again, to greet our longing eyes,
  His circuit hath begun.

Behold, each trembling, vassal star
  Is dimmed with reverent fear,
As, radiant in his glittering car,
  The day-god doth appear.

Oh god of light and love, in whose
  All-penetrative rays
Rejoice all creatures, hear our vows,
  Accept our songs of praise.

We come, this day, with special vows,
  And precious offerings bring;
This day, to thee, a holy house
  Doth consecrate our king.

Oh, on that work, propitious smile,
  His pious zeal hath planned,
And with thy glorious presence fill
  Our temple, and our land.

Ay, fill the years with mighty deeds
  Of our great lord and king,
Until all nations and all creeds
  Their cheerful homage bring.

And while the golden hours shall roll,
The gracious seasons glide,
Thy praise be hymned, from pole to pole,
Thy name be glorified.

After the hymn, came the rites of sacrifice. Never were they more beautiful or impressive. The victims were five snow-white oxen, ten sheep, and twenty lambs, bound to the altars by golden cords, and garlanded with gorgeous flowers. The orderly disposition of the altars, the scattered groups of priests, the glitter of the holy vessels and sacrificial weapons, the play of the many-colored flames, the clouds of fragrant incense, and, most beautiful of all, the graceful smoke-wreaths curling upward into the still air, and tinted with all hues, as they were pierced by the day-beams, gracious tokens of the smiles of the approving deity, all these things combined to form a picture of inexhaustible beauty. This service ended, a few brief words of thanksgiving were uttered by our reverend high-priest, and the audience dispersed, to prepare for the coming procession. This was formed at the temple of Ashur, and, after passing through the street of the Golden Gate, and beneath the new Arch of Triumph, ascended the platform by the northern entrance. It went round the northern, western, and southern façades of the palace, and so along the eastern front of the platform, to the temple, passing between the temporary structure I have before described and the statue of Semiramis. I can give you but a faint glimpse of its splendors. First came the bearers of the emblems of the heavenly hosts—spheres of gold and silver, borne aloft on poles with gay streamers, and conspicuous among them a magnificent crystal globe, placed within its richly embossed ring of gold, and dazzling all eyes as it slowly turned upon its golden axle—a fit image, truly, of the day-god. Then came the holy fires, on altars of silver, and surrounded by chanting priests, followed by the holy ones of our faith, arrayed in sumptuous new robes, and star-crowned caps, with attendants bearing the golden cups and tables. And then, the lovely youths, personators of the days, each with purple robe, and laurel wreath, worthy precursors of the votive chariot. This last was indescribably beautiful, with its graceful curves, its delicate, pearly hue within, the rich sculptures of its exterior, its glittering wheels, and yoke inlaid with jewels. It was drawn by twelve snow-white steeds. These, too, made a goodly show, with their bells and plumes, their braided manes, embroidered trappings, and shoes of gold; as did the grooms beside them, in their graceful caps and white garments, bearing golden wands. After the chariot came twelve maidens, charmingly grouped on a tastefully-decorated platform, all lovely, but each differing from the other in costume, attitude, and expression, admirably illustrating the party-colored hours of life, with their various burdens of joy or sorrow. This was, to me, the finest thing in the procession. Then came cars loaded with votive offerings of all kinds—fruits of the earth, and products of human skill; children all alike of the holy fire, whether they draw their life-blood directly from the heavenly rays, or take shape, mid pain and toil, at earthly forges. Of course, the gifts of the artificers, many and costly as they were, were quite lost sight of, in the superb display of fruits, and plants, and animals. I will not pretend to enumerate them. I will merely allude to the sacred tree of the silversmiths, whose graceful branches and exquisitely-wrought flowers caused quite a murmur of admiration among the beholders, and to the marvelous ingenuity of the kitchen-gardeners, in converting their seemingly unpromising materials into really beautiful stars, pyramids, rosettes, and fanciful devices of all sorts. I must also leave you to imagine the effect produced by the military portion of the procession which next followed, with its infinite variety of armor and costume; the admiration and awe with which it must have inspired the strangers present, and the joy of every loyal heart at beholding such evidences of the power and glory of the empire. After the troops came our nobles, with all their finery on. Beautiful were they to look upon, with their perfumed locks, their embroidered cloaks, gay tunics, and glittering jewels. Then came the Royal Guards, and at last, amid the acclamations and prostrations of the multitude, our glorious king seated in state in his magnificent chariot. He looked divinely in his flowing robes, inscribed all over with holy symbols, his mitre blazing with gems, his massive ear-rings and bracelets, and his golden girdle, clasped with diamonds. His left hand rested on his sword-hilt, while his right was raised, ever and anon, in act of benediction. To our dear friend Ithran was accorded the privilege of bearing the royal parasol on this occasion; its brilliant hues and embroidered curtain harmonizing admirably with the gorgeous standard, the rich armor, and all the other sumptuous appointments of the chariot. After the royal car came the chosen spearmen of the various legions, followed by cars containing the women and children of the royal household; their beauty worthily set off by their superb robes, and chaplets, and garlands of flowers. Finally came the reverend fathers of the Holy College, with a crowd of attendant priests, and scribes, and choristers, and bearers of the sacred books and vessels. It was almost noon when the procession reached its destination, and its different members had taken their appropriate places within and around the precincts of the temple.

Of the grand and imposing ceremony itself, I shall say but little. The moment of greatest interest was that in which the king, coming forth from the inner court, took his station before the high altar; no longer clad in his triumphal garments and jewels, but in the simple robes of sacrifice, the knotted cord around his waist, the mystic daggers in his girdle, the holy emblems about his neck, and bearing the sacred mace. After a slight pause, he knelt before the altar, the assembled multitude kneeling with him, and, in low but earnest tones, thus invoked the blessing of the god upon his work:

"Oh, thou Holy One, Fountain of Light, and Nourisher of all things; in whose sacred beams dwell and rejoice all creatures, from thy servant, man, down to the humblest worm, or weed of earth; Thou, who in thy benefits art so gracious, and in thy punishments so terrible! How shall we worthily set forth thy praises, and thy mighty deeds? Thou smilest, and lo, all nature reflects thy smile. Thou comest forth glorious in the morning, and behold the dew-drop sparkles with joy, the plant lifts up its drooping head, the flower renews its beauty, the bird pours forth its grateful song, the rivulet dances in the fields, the heart of the forest is stirred with gladness, the mountain is clad in robes of glory, the great sea rears his crest, exulting, and man riseth and goeth forth to his work rejoicing. Again, thou frownest in thine anger, and smitest us sore with thy terrible darts, and behold, we faint, and droop, and are ready to perish. Oh thou radiant and glorious one, ruler of the host of heaven; thou who marshalest the stars, and restrainest their wanderings, thyself obedient to the commands of the great Father of Lights, who made alike both thee and them, and who assigned unto thee thy glorious ministry, and unto them their courses, and their functions, and their mysterious influences, and who hast vouchsafed unto his chosen children of earth the grace and wisdom rightly to interpret their meanings, and so to guide the ways of men in accordance with their holy teachings; oh, thou blessed God, deign now to look down with favor upon thy servant, and upon all here assembled; and especially, bless thou this, the work of his hands, this holy temple which he this day sets apart for thy worship. Oh, wilt thou not smile upon it, and fill it with thy glorious presence? And do thou now, in token of thy acceptance of our offering, send down thy gracious messenger from above, that he may kindle the sacred fire upon this altar, before which thy servant now bends low in adoration; that holy fire which is never more to be extinguished on earth, but which, intrusted to the keeping of thy pious servants, is to burn pure and serene, through all the coming ages. And oh, as that flame is kindled upon this altar, so may the flame of pious zeal burn brightly in the hearts of all here present; and as that fire is to be fed with choicest food, by faithful hands administered, so may our souls be nourished and sustained by the pure food of heavenly wisdom. Oh, look down graciously, now, and accept the house we consecrate to thee; accept our votive rites and gifts; bless the priesthood this day set apart for thy service, and may our prayers, and songs, and sacrifices find favor in thy sight. And unto thee, O blessed God, and unto the holy Twelve who sit in council, and unto the Father of all, be endless praise and glory."

After the prayer came the solemn chant of invocation, at the conclusion of which, the reverend archflamen held up the mystic glass to receive the holy rays, and as the flame burst into life, and danced upon the altar, the harps struck up their joyous notes, and the choir sang that famous hymn of thanksgiving, so dear and familiar to us all, beginning—

Rejoice, rejoice, he hath heard our cry,
Our gracious God, from his throne on high!
See, how the golden flame aspires—
Bright offspring of the eternal fires.

It was given with fine effect, all present joining in the last verse:

With gifts, with vows, with blood of lambs,
And fervent prayers, and holy psalms,
Our children's children here shall sing
Thy glorious praise, O heavenly king!

Then followed the presentation of the gifts, the consecration of the priests, and finally, the immolation of the victims; all of which ceremonies were performed with a splendor, precision, and solemnity, most commendable, and worthy of the august occasion. The entire services lasted about three hours, and then, after a welcome interval of repose, came the beautiful and impressive rites, at sunset: the scene, a magnificent pavilion, erected immediately behind the temple, and adorned with sumptuous velvet hangings of all hues; looking, indeed, as you approached it, almost as grand and gorgeous as the spectacle of which it was the emblem. The company assembled was not so large as that of the early morning service, but the picture itself was even more brilliant and imposing. I shall not undertake to paint it, or to describe the ceremonies, merely giving you the closing hymn :

And now our task is o'er,
  Which thou, O God, this day hast blest :
Behold, thy fiery car once more
  Glows in the golden west.

In robes of splendor clad,
  Midst clouds that bear thy gorgeous train,
Thou goest other skies to glad,
  And climes beyond the main.

To bathe in blissful light
  The slumbering towns, the silent towers,
Revive the fields, the birds delight,
  And ope the eyes of flowers.

Again the sleepers called,
  Awake, and sing their Maker's praise,
While night's pale spectres flee appalled
  Before thy searching rays.

Alike the demon train,
  Who vex the curtained sleep with wicked dreams,
And the gay sprites that haunt the lover's brain,
  Are driven before thy beams.

And now, as morning wears,
  Each scene of varied life behold,
From monarch, on his throne of cares,
  To shepherd at the fold.

Again, thy journey done,
  Thou leavest them to night and rest;
Again thy servants, heavenly Sun,
  In thy bright smiles are blest.

Now, as thy parting rays
  Faint glimmer in the silent air,
Once more we chant our hymn of praise,
  And lowly bow in prayer.

After the evening service, there was a grand banquet in the Southern Hall of the palace, the superb appointments of which fitly corresponded with the other splendors of our festival. So, at least, thought our good friend Clœlius, next whom I had the honor of reclining at table. The entertainment broke up at an early hour, and I was right glad to get back to my own quiet house, after a day of so much fatigue and excitement.

Of the temple itself I need not speak to you, who are already so familiar with its plan and its details. The ornaments that have been added to it, both without and within, since you left, worthily carry out the grand ideas of the architect. There is but one feeling here, in the minds of king, priests, and people—that of unbounded satisfaction. Its vast size, graceful proportions, the harmony of its colors, the fine finish of its paintings and sculptures, and its rare felicity of position, all combine to make it, at once, an ornament to the metropolis, and a precious addition to the monuments of our faith. It would take many days to study out all its merits, from the grand forms that guard its portals, down to the minute ornaments of its ceilings. I spent several hours in it to-day, and was deeply impressed with the vast amount of hard, faithful labor that has been expended upon it; not a beam, stone, or brick, however minute, but what worthily contributes, in the way of form, color, or inscription, to the grand whole. And then, the convenience of all its arrangements—its commodious stalls for the victims, the abundance of its cisterns, its admirably planned store-rooms, and robing-rooms, and treasury, its cheerful apartments for the priests and students, its spacious refectory, and choice little library, and the quiet and beautiful garden attached to it; altogether, the impression left on the mind of the visitor is most agreeable. I know several of the members of its priesthood; worthy and learned men, with pure and loyal hearts. It could not be in better keeping; while the rich estates with which it has been endowed, will afford abundant means of keeping the temple in perfect order, and of preserving, unimpaired, the splendor and decorum of its services. May the gods smile upon it, and may the long ages to come behold it here, beautiful as ever, and its ministers faithful to their holy calling!

But it is quite time to bring my long letter to an end. I hope you will like my new seal. I have only received it this morning from the engravers, and this is the first epistle to which I have appended it, since my appointment. I can't help saying that I think the border exceedingly tasteful, though I *did* design it. With best love to Zethar, and all dear friends at Babylon, I am your ever-loving

TELASSAR.

LETTER VI.

TELASSAR TO MEMUCAN.

PARDON me, my dear friend, for so long neglecting to reply to your last most agreeable letter. And to say truth, I have not had my usual good excuse for my silence, the last few days having been comparatively free from official duties.

There is but little of public interest to communicate to you. Our good general and his brave son returned, a few days since, from their brief but brilliant campaign. The youth has, indeed, greatly distinguished himself, and has been warmly commended by His Majesty. His beauty and prowess are quite the talk of the town, and, no doubt, many a young damsel's heart is aching, at this moment, on his account. The king, with his usual promptness, has set apart a superb chamber in the northern front of the palace, for the adequate illustration of the events of the expedition. The stones are already in the hands of the sculptors, and I have been instructed to prepare appropriate inscriptions.

The king of Armenia having at length fully complied with the conditions imposed by himself, and accepted by His Majesty, the young prince left us yesterday. We were sorry to part with him, he having won all hearts by his gentleness and intelligence. His accomplishments are quite beyond his years, and he handles alike the bow and the reed, with rare adroitness. With proper training, I have no doubt he would ripen into a great and good king, but the court of Armenia, I fear, is but a poor school for the virtues. His Majesty gave him, at parting, a beautiful horse, and an exquisitely wrought necklace, and dismissed him with a speech, the words and manner of which betokened a hearty interest in the youth's welfare.

In some of my recent letters I have spoken to you of pleasant interviews which I have had with Clœlius, the Roman ambassador, now absent on a visit to the court of King Deioces. Since then, I have made the acquaintance of another stranger here; a very different kind of man, truly; one far more distinguished in his own country, and not altogether unknown to us of Assyria. I speak of the Grecian Archilochus, the illustrious poet, whom some of his admirers rank, even now, with their famous Homer himself. I first met him at the house of our good neighbor, the chatty Menahem. His visit here is one of mere curiosity, and as I infer from his own account of it, must have been quite unpremeditated. I hardly know how to describe him. He is rather a small, slender man, dressed with great elaborateness, and with a countenance full of intelligence and animation. It is furrowed with wrinkles, not so much the work of time as of thought and feeling, and the many hardships of a life of strange vicissitudes. His brow is lofty and noble, his dark eye full of lustre, his nose strongly developed, and of great flexibility, while his mouth is quite a language, of itself, so marvelously does it express all the varied emotions of the man. His hair is almost white, though he has not yet seen fifty summers. He has a voice of great compass and sweetness, talks fast, with many gestures, and appears to have all languages at his fingers' ends; a memory, too, which grasps, holds, and reproduces all things at will, a marvelous play of wit (so far, at least, as I can follow it, for at times it flies quite beyond my ken), and a seemingly inexhaustible store of anecdotes, derived from his large and varied experience of life. You can imagine how entertaining and instructive the talk of such a man must be; and yet, there is occasionally a tone of bitterness and sarcasm about it, that mars the otherwise delightful impression made by it; a bold, reckless way, also, of speaking of sacred things, that grates on an Assyrian ear. He is one, evidently, who, midst many triumphs, has, likewise, had many hard struggles with fortune, and with his fellow-men, and who has not taken the severe lessons of the gods in the right spirit. I have derived from him much curious information concerning the manners, customs, dress, cookery, and amusements of his countrymen, as well as their religion and form of government, in so few respects like, in so many utterly unlike, our own. I cannot pretend to give you any adequate idea of the conversation of Archilochus, but will briefly notice some few of the topics, about which we have interchanged ideas; more particularly during a long talk which we had together yesterday.

After expressing unbounded astonishment at the power and prosperity of the empire, and the magnificence of the metropolis, which, he said, far exceeded all images he had framed of them, or stories that he had heard about them, he proceeded to illustrate in a rapid and brilliant, though somewhat desultory, way, some of the more remarkable points of contrast between the two nations. What first and most struck a Greek here, he said, was the profound submission, the unquestioning obedience, of the people to their monarch; the utter abnegation of all right to an opinion, even by the educated few, on all matters of faith and government; so different from Athens and Sparta (he quoted these, as being the two principal members of the confederacy of which Greece is composed); in the former of which states, the idea of monarchy had been rejected for some centuries, the people meeting, and electing their own officers of all kinds, and, for brief periods, while in the latter, though the name of king was still retained, his authority was virtually taken from him, by the popular assemblies on the one hand, and, on the other, by a peculiar censorship, which even went so far as to dictate to him the color of the robes he should wear, and the qualities of the woman he should marry. He went on to describe these same popular assemblies, their various kinds, and modes of meeting, and passing laws, and the perfect equality which prevailed in them; the humblest and poorest member having the same right of voting, and the same freedom of speech allowed him, as the noblest and most opulent, and in Sparta, as the king himself. In these assemblies all subjects, save the holy mysteries of their faith, were discussed without restraint, and especially all subjects connected with money. Not a drachma could be raised in the way of tax or tribute, or for any purpose of war or peace, without the full consent of these meetings, and after the most ample discussion. (What would his majesty say to this? The idea, that a poor wretch, with hardly a tunic to his back, should enjoy privileges, which he does not concede even to tributary kings!) Archilochus recited some of the laws passed in these assemblies, many of them being very ancient, and those pertaining to morals being put into verse, that they may be more deeply engraved on the hearts of the people. Some of the simpler ones, he says, are chanted daily by the children in the schools. He first gave them in the original, and then, with wonderful facility and grace, in Assyrian. Many of them certainly seemed to me most impolitic and absurd; others again, alike wise and beautiful. Those treating of marriage, parent and child, and the relation of debtor and creditor, I was especially struck with, as being both just and admirably expressed; and there were others, leveled at idlers, and non taxpayers, that were full of pith, and pungency, and severity. I am sorry they do not live in my memory, for they are well worth repeating. Archilochus has promised, however, to copy for me some of the more striking and characteristic of them.

Among the remarkable institutions of Athens, he gave an interesting account of a court of justice, as old, he said, as the nation. It is composed of some twenty of the most venerable and virtuous of the citizens, and meets on certain nights of each month, under circumstances of great dignity and solemnity, in an open court, on the brow of a hill near the city, and deals with murder, impiety, and other high crimes. His description of it was very graphic. The altar in the midst, the group of aged judges, with their silver beards, and flowing white garments, the glare of the torches, the gleam of the armor of the guard who watch over their deliberations, the deep gloom in which both the criminal and his accuser are enshrouded (the court being unwilling to look upon the face of either, lest they should thereby be biased in their judgment), the absence of all vain words and idle rhetoric, and the solemn formula in which the presiding judge pronounces sentence, invoking the holy stars above them to bear witness to the justice of their decision, all these circumstances combined to form a most impressive picture, and certainly a very novel one to an Assyrian.

He had a great deal to say, also, about the institutions at Sparta, many of which differ almost as much from those of Athens as both do from our own. It was evident that he had a far higher opinion of the Athenian mind, and manners, and laws, than of those of the rival state. At the same time, he spoke in glowing words of the founder of the Spartan code, who lived about two centuries ago (Lycurgus, if I mistake not, he called him), and who must have been a man of rare virtues, and, with all his errors of judgment, a deep and subtle thinker. It would be difficult to imagine a state of society more directly opposite to our own, than that of Sparta, as he described it. Their principal city, it seems, is small and clumsily built, unadorned with fine dwellings or public buildings, and unprotected by walls. The inhabitants, though naturally well-formed and handsome, appear to set no value on the amenities, or even decencies, of life. They go about in garments alike filthy and scanty, and without any during the heats of summer. They despise sandals, even the women, and are averse to ablutions. They dine together at long tables, king and all, without distinction, and the fare, as Archilochus described it, is such as we would hardly set before galley-slaves. Their language is as unpicturesque as their costume, and they take especial pride, he says, in their brief and blunt answers to all questions. They have periodical distributions of all the property in the state, landed and personal, in which all share alike, with some slight exception in the king's favor. This, and the privilege of commanding the army in time of war, and of putting an additional story on his house, if needful, constitute the entire distinction between him and his subjects. Their treatment of children, especially boys, is very rigorous. While their meals are few and scanty, their floggings are many and plentiful. In short, they are exposed to all manner of hardships, insomuch that, while many die under them, the survivors acquire a degree of intrepidity and fortitude that makes them invincible as soldiers. Among their strange institutions, they have what Archilochus calls their annual flogging-day. On this day, the boys are all brought up into the court before the temple of one of their goddesses, and lashed with great severity—their parents accompanying them, and encouraging them to bear the blows cheerfully. To cry or wince is disgraceful, while they who are silent and serene under the treatment are rewarded with laurel-crowns and acclamations. A fat boy, it seems, is looked upon with peculiar suspicion, and is flogged faithfully till he loses his roundness. The freedom which they allow their young women is another strange feature in their system. (In this respect, the usages of the Athenians are far more like our own, according to Archilochus.) They appear in public without veils, and sometimes almost in a state of nudity; they dance, sing, box, wrestle, throw quoits, and run races, in short, partake in all manly exercises, in order that they may thereby acquire a hardiness of constitution, which they may transmit to their children.

One very remarkable precept in the code of Lycurgus reads as follows: *Thou shalt steal; thou shalt not be found out.* I am not jesting. Archilochus has seen it, inscribed on innumerable tablets, and engraven on the pillars of their market-places. The dominant idea in the mind of this lawgiver appears to have been to make his people soldiers, and not merely brave and enduring, but active, cunning, and vigilant ones; and these latter qualities the practice of theft seemed to him to be the most obvious and thorough mode of developing. Such is our friend's, not altogether satisfactory, explanation of this strange law. But if you open your eyes at it, in amazement, what *will* you say to the statement I am now about to make, namely, that the practice of parent-killing has prevailed from time immemorial, among this most peculiar people? Up to the age of threescore years and ten, they, like the rest of the world, honor, cherish, and obey the authors of their being; but the moment that point is reached, they turn upon and slaughter them—considering them as so many encumbrances to be got rid of, impediments in the way of active duty. And to show how habit hardens the hearts, and perverts the ideas of men, there is no thought of resistance or cry for mercy on the one hand, or show of pity on the other. The old people are put out of the way, to quote the words of Archilochus, just as worthless weeds would be removed from a well-ordered garden, or withered branches from a consecrated grove. He added, that he had more than once conversed with Spartans who had killed both father and mother that same morning before breakfast, and who appeared not only resigned and serene, but positively cheerful and hilarious, by the time the dinner-trumpet sounded. I watched him narrowly, when he made this last remark; for, to say truth, his irony is so subtle at times, and his manner so bewildering, that I can hardly tell whether he be in jest or in earnest. To be sure, that telltale mouth of his is apt to betray him, in the midst of a piece of mystification; but, on this occasion, I fear that his words were too true. I dare not trust myself with any comments on such a custom as this, and can only hope that no other land beneath the sun is polluted by it. I ought to add, by the way, that Archilochus is not very well-disposed towards the Spartans, he having been, as he told me, grossly insulted during his last visit there. It seems that our friend, some years ago, as he very candidly confessed, left a battle-field rather prematurely, and without his buckler—moving off with a rapidity quite unworthy of a poet of his reputation. The news of this unfortunate affair preceded him to Sparta, where, as you will imagine from what I have written above, such an offense is considered far more heinous than murder itself. He was received accordingly, and the indignities, then offered him, may have insensibly colored his descriptions.

Another characteristic trait of us, Assyrians, as set forth by our Greek friend, was our antipathy to innovations—not merely a contented and placid acquiescence in things as they are, but a positive aversion to all changes, no matter how reasonable or desirable, either in religion, or arts, or laws. Every Ninevite seemed to take it for granted, that the position assigned him by the gods was the right one, from the great King and High Priest himself, down to the humblest tiller of the fields. The thought of ever altering his place in the grand procession of life, or of finding another and better one for his children after him, never seemed to occur to him, or, if it did, was instantly dismissed from his mind. Everything that he saw here, bore emphatic witness to this love of letting things alone. The city itself, with all its magnificence, was, he doubted not, a mere copy, on a grand scale, of the Nineveh of three thousand years ago. The walls were expanded, the palaces and temples were vaster and more adorned with images, the parks more capacious and more enriched with the spoils of nature and of nations; and yet, the scene, how essentially the same, in all important particulars! The same unequal distribution of burdens and prizes, the same irresponsible and unquestioned autocracy, the same monopoly of learning by the priesthood, the same exclusive enjoyment, by the nobility, of all the high offices of the state; the very language itself the same, with its pompous and picturesque phrases, its formal preambles and repetitions, and its alphabet, encumbered with superfluous and complicated letters. And the Nineveh of three thousand years to come, inexpressibly grand and splendid as it will be, yet will it not be essentially the same marvelous tale it is to-day, told only to a larger circle of listeners? Will not the subjects of those far-off ages obey their monarch with the same silent promptness as they now do; the husbandmen plow their masters' lands with the same old-fashioned plows; the artificers work with the same tools for the same scanty wages; the children puzzle over the same tough spelling-books; the architects build after the same plans; the priests chant the same old hymns to the same old music? He believed it: such was the spirit of the people—the same, yesterday, to-day, and forever. Archilochus illustrated this point very minutely and fancifully, and with hisusual rapidity of utterance. I found it difficult to keep up with him. "How different," he finally added, "all this, from our restless, discontented, inquisitive, speculative, all-trying Athenians! They never *will* let things alone; are forever making and mending their laws, and changing their rulers; claiming full liberty, not only of criticising, but of lampooning them and hissing them in the very market-places, if they do not act in accordance with their caprices. Life at Athens, so far from being the pompous and orderly procession that it is here, with its iron rules of precedence, is far more like the tumult and confusion of a chance-gathered crowd. People are forever changing places; the ruler of to-day may be the humble citizen of to-morrow, while, on the other hand, the poorest and most obscure Athenian may become chief archon, provided he reveal a capacity to govern." (He mentioned the names of several who had either been themselves, or were the sons of, bakers and butchers, and potters, ay, of very tinkers, and who had afterwards filled the highest offices in the state.) "New opinions are constantly appearing and disappearing on all subjects—social, domestic, artistic, religious. Our holy mysteries are not, indeed, discussed in our public assemblies, but are freely examined, and commented on in private; nay, in the streets, you often hear sentiments about them, which pass unchecked and unrebuked, but which here would instantly cost him his head, who uttered them. Novelties, novelties!—these are what the people love, and must have, from a new theory of the universe, down to a new tie of a sandal."

Archilochus spoke somewhat of the innovations in language made by his countrymen. The hundred letters of the alphabet, which they received from us, as you are aware, they have reduced to four-and-twenty; and they have not merely dismissed the superfluous ones, but have rearranged and simplified the forms of those which they have retained—or, as he expressed it, put them in trim and orderly array for active mental service—thereby materially aiding the operations of the student and the thinker, and, at the same time, helping the poor school-boy cheerily along the thorny path of knowledge—"thorny, indeed," said he, "in its beginnings; but oh, to what lovely flowers and precious fruits finally leading us!" He explained to me, also, some ingenious contrivances whereby they render the inflection of their words a far less tedious and far more philosophical process than it is with us;

and how, by the use of short and expressive particles, they avoid those circumlocutions which so encumber our language, and which render its grammar so formidable to learners. Their system of numerals, too, as he illustrated it, is much more compact and beautiful than ours; they have made some improvements likewise, in arithmetic, "which your people," said he, "might advantageously, but, of course, never *will*, adopt."

On the subject of religion, he said much that was interesting—much that offended alike my national prejudices, and my sense of propriety. Sad and strange liberties, truly, have these same Greeks taken with our pantheon—dismissing old gods, introducing new ones, at pleasure. Worse than this, they have not even spared the ever-holy and mystic Twelve themselves, but have invested them with most unseemly attributes—have given them all the appetites and passions of mortals—have sung and painted them, now quarreling over their cups, now contending for the favors of goddesses—at one time exchanging opprobrious epithets at their council boards, at another actually coming down and taking part in the battles of men. Worst of all, their best wits, their most distinguished poets, so says Archilochus, have adopted these sad perversions; have wedded them to beautiful and melodious verse;

have clothed them with alluring and seductive imagery, and so rendered them dear and familiar to the people. Ah, if *such* be the results of innovation, thank heaven that I am an Assyrian! How different from our own pure faith! Our religion may have been cruel and intolerant, at times, too impatient of contradiction, too fond of propagating its tenets by the sword, too much encumbered, if you will, with gorgeous and costly rites, and inexplicable mysteries; but it has, at least, been a chaste religion. Quaint and fanciful as its services are, at times, they are yet uniformly decorous, and you might search in vain, through all the temples of the empire, for a single indecent image or inscription. But I will not dwell on this part of our guest's conversation. Another institution utterly unknown to us of Assyria, namely, the games of Greece (of which I had some vague and imperfect notions, derived from casual travelers), Archilochus described very minutely and graphically. They are held, it seems, once every four years, at midsummer, near a famous sacred grove, in a lovely valley, watered by a noble river, and are visited by hundreds of thousands, both spectators and combatants, from all the towns and villages of the land. They consist of all manner of mental and bodily exercises, and every Greek, no matter what his origin, if he be of good character, and has undergone a certain amount of preliminary training, is allowed to enter the lists. The judges are chosen from the most intelligent and upright of the citizens, and are sworn into office with peculiar solemnities. The games last several days, during which period every one present is upon his good behavior. It is emphatically a friendly gathering, a season of peace and good-will. Here old feuds are forgotten, old friendships are renewed; and they who, all the rest of their lives, may be ill-mannered, and dissolute, and abandoned, make it a point of honor to restrain their evil passions on this occasion, and to wear at least the semblance of gentleness and decorum. Such a solemn festival is it considered—such a bond of union to the people—the great crowning event of the national experience. And what, think you, are the prizes of excellence? But one is ever awarded to the victor, no matter in what department, and that, a simple crown of olive. More than once have the brows of Archilochus been bound with these wreaths of conquest; and it is evident that he sets far more store by these poor, withered memorials, than if they were so many crowns of gold, blazing with jewels. "That was in my younger and happier days," said he, "ere the gods were so unkind to me; when my name was dear, not only to my native Paros, but to all its sister isles." (What these reverses have been, that have thus saddened and embittered our friend, I know not, though I infer, from hints that he has dropped, that disappointments in love grieve him far more than any losses of fame or fortune.) "But these," he added, "are my greatest consolations in my misfortunes, these precious evidences of my former victories in art; and every true Greek, that has been thus honored, feels as I do. An Olympic garland he values as the richest ornament of his house—the best bequest that he can leave to his children." When men talk thus, you can readily imagine the effect which such an institution must, in time, have upon the character of a people—what a spirit of emulation it must arouse—what immense moral and physical results it must lead to. Similar games, Archilochus says, are daily springing up all over the land, and are sowing the seeds, he thinks, of a glorious future for the nation. "And who knows," he added, "but what, some day, even you, old-fashioned, routine-loving, solemn, obedient Assyrians, may open your eyes to the manifest advantages of such gatherings?"

But you may think me tedious, perhaps, and wonder why I should go into all these details about a people comparatively so small, obscure, and remote, and who will probably never come into contact with the empire, save in the character of humble tributaries. True, nor does Archilochus himself think otherwise, or that the sword of Greece will ever be raised in rebellion against the great king. It is not the physical, but the intellectual future of his nation, that he looks forward to with such confidence. Indeed, he is as full of this idea, as good, visionary king Numa, of whom I wrote to you in previous letters, is of the future military glory and world-wide dominion of his little, far-off, infant Rome. When once fairly started on this topic, Archilochus seems to forget all his troubles and griefs, to lay aside all levity and sarcasm, his face flushes, his eye kindles, his whole form expands, his voice pours out its deep, noble notes, his whole air and manner are that of a true poet and prophet. "The future of Greece," said he, "were it written in letters of light on yonder sky, I could not see it more clearly. I look along the coming ages, and there rise before my dazzled vision, whole groups and constellations of genius, the like of which earth hath never seen—poets, painters, sculptors, architects, statesmen, philosophers, who are to enrich the world with precious thoughts innumerable, embodied in every grand and beautiful form—to build the lofty verse, to rear the holy pile, to pour forth the sweet hymn of thanksgiving, to breathe life into the divine image, to weave wise codes and construct new systems of government, to unfold the mysteries of the outer world, to interpret anew the laws of mind, and to read, with searching eyes, the deep, sad secrets of the heart. Ay, the seed is sown, which a few centuries are to ripen into this magnificent harvest. These glorious games, these vast school-houses, these educators of the people, these parents of the virtues and the graces, they are to be the blessed instruments of the gods, in working out these wonders. Already have we the promise of these things in the virtues and achievements of our countrymen, in the sublime devotion of Codrus, the stern wisdom of Lycurgus, in the soul-stirring odes of Tyrtaeus, the vivid pictures of Hesiod, the sublime sentiments of Homer, precious pledges all of the golden days to come."

But my imperfect report does no justice to this part of his conversation. I wish you could have heard him. You would have called him wild and visionary, perhaps; but the music of his voice, the ardor of his manner, the earnestness of his gestures, the whole tone of passion and poetic fervor that pervaded his speech, would have delighted you. A strange, rich, interesting character, indeed; full of puzzles and contrasts, and requiring a much deeper analysis than my scanty acquaintance with him enables me to give.

I could not resist asking him for a specimen of his poetical compositions, and particularly of those which won for him his crowns at Olympia. He at once complied, and taking Zeresh's harp, played a simple prelude, and then chanted a hymn to Hercules, which he considers his masterpiece, and which (a most rare compliment) he was called on to recite three times during the same celebration. Of course only a word here and there was intelligible to me, but the mere sound of the language itself was most agreeable to the ear. As I was about to express my regret that I could not honor his performance with a more intelligent admiration, he, with wonderful ease and grace, forthwith translated the piece into right excellent and sonorous Assyrian. I was alike astonished and charmed. True, his conceptions of the god are widely different from ours, and his interpretations of the symbols of his worship. Amid all his mighty works, he makes him strangely human, and endows him with a full share of infirmities and passions. Such a rendering would not, of course, be tolerated for a moment, in our temples, shocking, as it does, all the prejudices of a literal and sober-minded Assyrian worshiper. And yet, there were passages in it of wonderful power and beauty; superb descriptions both of people and scenery, striking comparisons, finely managed ebbs and flows of feeling, and an admirably elaborated climax in the closing invocation, that quite took me by storm.

With the same willingness and facility did he give me versions in Assyrian, of several other of his poems. His muse is a most versatile one, truly ; now a pious strain, now an heroic, or an amorous one ; and he then would recite an epigram of rare humor and pungency, and at times, it must be owned, somewhat bordering on indecency. There was a hiss and sting, too, about some of them, that was, indeed, terrible, and I could not help pitying the poor wretches they were aimed at. Others again, leveled more particularly at inconstant beauties, were recited by him with an animation and zest, that only confirmed me in the belief that he has been shamefully jilted, in his earlier days, by some spoiled beauty, and has never forgiven her for it. He concluded his recitations by giving us some truly magnificent passages from Homer.

How long our brilliant and eccentric guest is to remain with us, and whither he goes from Nineveh, I know not. I shall not fail to see as much of him as my duties at the palace will allow; for it is a long time since I have seen a man so enriched with accomplishments, and with all his infirmities, so true and genial at bottom. But I have reached the edge of my papyrus, and, without another word, must bid you farewell.

TELASSAR.

LETTER VII.

TELASSAR TO MEMUCAN.

Your letter of the tenth, my dear friend, was received yesterday, having been just five days coming. Its predecessor was more than eleven days on the road. How is it, that your Babylonian couriers are so irregular?

I proceed to answer some of your questions relative to the discoveries near Resen. You ask me, in the first place, as to the extent of those discoveries; secondly, how far I agree with you in thinking that they bear witness to great changes (and those not for the better) in the language, art, and religion of the empire; thirdly, why it is that such monuments of national power have not been rescued long ago, from the neglect, decay, and oblivion into which they have fallen; and, finally, what are the king's intentions with regard to them? I will answer you to the best of my ability, on all these points.

And first, you will be pleased to learn that the

excavations are nearly completed, a few small chambers only in the palace of Sardanapalus being unexplored; that the tower has been opened, and its vaulted and richly-painted chamber (in which its royal builder vainly hoped to repose) has been found in admirable preservation; and, moreover, that, to the south and east of the tower, two temples have been discovered, each dedicated to our holy Merodach; small, but highly-adorned structures, and containing some interesting objects and inscriptions. I have visited the place several times lately—once or twice in company with his majesty. I shall send you with this, several drawings, including the plans of the temples, and the chamber of sepulture of the tower, and others, as soon as completed. These will be far more satisfactory to you than any long descriptions of my own. It would seem that the temples, both dedicated by Sardanapalus, must have survived the ruin of the neighboring palace. One of them has evidently been destroyed by fire, of which there are also some traces in the other, but none whatever in the palace itself. It would appear that the audacious rebels, while showing no mercy to the royal mansion, yet had enough of pious fear lingering in their wicked hearts to deter them from desecrating those of the gods, and that some after-casualty must have overtaken them. Of the historical records that have been found in all the buildings, many are quite valuable. The tablets and cylinders have been removed to the Archive Chamber, and the inscriptions on the slabs and monoliths have been carefully copied. Two admirable statues of Sardanapalus—one quite small, the other somewhat larger than life, and both in good preservation, found in front of one of the temples—are now in the Gallery of Antiquities, and a third, in high relief; a fine work, though greatly injured by the flames. I need not call your attention to the rich decorations and elaborate paintings in the tomb-chamber, as set forth in one of the accompanying colored drawings. Some of the sculptures of the temples are exceedingly quaint and fanciful. The drawing, which I have marked *No.* 16, is a faithful copy of one of the most remarkable of them. I think you will agree with me in calling it a very striking illustration of the conflict between the good and evil principle; especially the figure of the evil one, whose vast proportions and varied and hideous deformities most aptly portray the colossal, and complicated, and inexplicable ills and sufferings that form so large a part of the discipline of life. Some very spirited delineations of the divine Oannes, also, will not fail to call forth your pious enthusiasm.

But I must proceed to your second inquiry; and

to answer it candidly, it appears to me that your hasty and partial examinations, on your way to Babylon, have betrayed you into much stronger language than you would now use after a deliberate and thorough survey of the place. I cannot see those alarming evidences of deterioration that you speak of, either in the national art, or literature, or religion. These newly-discovered edifices certainly testify to some changes in these respects, and demonstrate that we men of Assyria are not so thoroughly unimpressible and immutable a people as travelers always call us, and we are so proud of calling ourselves. Our language, it must be owned, has changed since those days, and bears unmistakable marks of the Median conquest. It certainly is far more like the Babylonian than it was three centuries ago, both in its construction and phraseology, and in the very forms of some of its letters. There is a certain terseness and simplicity in these old records, which we do not find in those of to-day. Their sententious gravity and graphic descriptions are more agreeable to the scholar, than the long, unmanageable, detail-loving narratives of our own scribes. On the other hand, however, these latter records are enriched with many useful and noble words and phrases, which are wanting in the elder ones; precious evidences of our enlarged conquests, and ever-increasing intercourse with other nations: so that what we have lost in the way of simplicity and graphic power, is more than recompensed to us, by the greater abundance, both of facts and ideas. And so in art; I admire as heartily as you do the sculptures of the palace of Sardanapalus, the spirit, and movement, and expression of the figures; and I agree with you in thinking that too many of our modern artists are apt to overlook these higher virtues of art, in their attention to unimportant particulars; that they overload their works with a multitude of figures and objects, and are inclined to sacrifice the proprieties of the story they illustrate, to the idle display of their own executive power On the other hand, again, this very profusion of details makes their works far more instructive and suggestive to the student of history than the older ones. But these faults are by no means universal, and surely you can recall many noble compositions, in the storied chambers of our palace, and in those of the palace of King Sargon, which combine the merits of both eras—the spirit and fidelity of the one, with the fullness of details and minute technical excellences of the other.

Still less can I see, as you do, any evidence borne by these discoveries, to a decline in the purity of our faith, or in the fervor of its votaries. I see, certainly, some additions to the objects of our worship; a few ideas (and those grand and beautiful ones), incorporated from the creeds of neighboring nations, and more particularly from that of Egypt; a few unimportant modifications in the robes of some of our deities, and in the emblems which they bear; and a far more widely-diffused worship of the holy fire. But I certainly do not infer from this last circumstance, as you appear to do, that, in our more general adoration of the earthly, we have lost sight of the heavenly; that we do not bow with the same pious reverence as ever, before those blessed lights above, do not acknowledge as humbly, those precious mysteries, of which they are the types Oh no, on the contrary, I see about me, daily (and all the more clearly, now that my official duties compel me to know and record these things), ten thousand evidences that our religion was never so flourishing as now, so enriched with precious thoughts and holy symbols, so abounding in splendid temples and ceremonials, so watched over by a devoted priesthood, so dear and venerable in the eyes of the people. Never were the Assyrians so ready to live in accordance with, so eager to fight, and, if need be, to die for their blessed faith, as now. Thus you see, my dear friend, we differ essentially on these points; so far from having any disheartening thoughts in connection with these discoveries, they only inspire me with renewed pride and gratitude, by reminding me how much the empire has gained in power and renown, since the days of Sardanapalus. In a word, his palace and that of our great king, seem to me most fitly to illustrate their respective eras; and, as Assyria is far more vast and formidable now than she was then, with more armies in her pay, more nations under her wing, and a hundred-fold more enriched, alike with the spoils of war and the products of her own industry, so in the house of her monarch, we find a corresponding increase of proportions, and splendors, and treasures, and of those monuments that are to tell her proud story worthily to the coming ages.

But you ask, in the third place, how it is, that these buildings have not been restored long since, but have been suffered thus to perish, and pass out of the sight and memory of men? And, moreover, why the annals of the empire are so exceedingly meagre and unsatisfactory in their accounts of them? At first blush, it certainly seems strange enough, that within the walls of our magnificent and populous Nineveh, such a palace as this should have been slumbering under ground for so many generations, and that the merest accident should have been the means of restoring it to the light of day; and again, that, when found, it should be so entirely its own chronicler. And yet, these things seem to explain themselves pretty satisfactorily, when we come to reflect upon them. Look at the facts, for a moment. And first, consider the success that crowned the arms of the Median usurper, aided as he was by that accursed traitor-priest, the ever-infamous Belesis; consider the terrible destruction that they wrought here, and the long years of insolent and cruel tyranny that they inflicted upon us; consider the protracted and bloody struggles that ensued before the final extermination of the invaders, and the reëstablishment of the empire; and then, the brief, busy, and troublous reigns of the first monarchs of our new dynasty—what wars they had to wage, what tributaries to overawe, what troops to raise and discipline, what strong-holds to repair, what conspiracies to quell, what ceaseless pains and anxieties they underwent, in relaying deep and broad the foundations of the empire—yes, even unto the days of the glorious Sargon himself. What a care-laden no less than triumphant reign was his, too! What time had he to brood over, much less restore, the ruins of the past, when the present was so crowded with duties and excitements? Think of his manifold benefits to Assyria—the new walls he gave her cities, his splendid agricultural experiments, his improvement of the navigation of our noble rivers, and above all, the restoration and enlargement of those magnificent canals—the wonder and pride of the old empire; think of these things, and tax him not with apathy, or neglect of his ancestors. And will not the same reasoning apply with even greater force to the reign of our own mighty king, the all-conquering Sennacherib, whose holy banners wave alike over the sea of the rising sun, and the great sea of the setting sun? What hours has he had to spare from his numberless expeditions, and victories, and treaties, his mighty works all over the empire, and in his beloved capital, which he has endowed with so many noble monuments, temples, and palaces, and fortifications, and aqueducts, and fountains, and statues innumerable; what hours, I ask again, has he had, to give to reveries amidst the tombs of his forefathers, or to disturb the slumbers of their grass-grown palaces? Do not these facts, thus briefly glanced at, sufficiently explain the seeming neglect of which you complain? There is another consideration also, which we ought not to forget, in this connection—the tower, which the builder of this palace erected, with such care and cost, for his final resting-place, was destined never to receive his august remains.

Had it been otherwise, how dear and reverend a monument it would have been in the eyes of the nation—how faithfully preserved! And, in that pious care, no doubt, would have been included the restoration of those twin temples which he reared, and the rebuilding of the imperial mansion itself. But as it was, the vacant tomb only made the desolation more desolate, and increased that natural aversion which every man feels for reëstablishing his home, be it gilded dome or straw-thatched cot, on the very spot where misery and ruin have overtaken it. All things considered, then, is it strange that the kings of the new dynasty should have reared their palaces elsewhere, or that these edifices should have thus fallen into decay and oblivion? The silence of the historian, too, concerning them, and his meagre accounts of the times in which they flourished, are they not as easily explained by the loss of materials implied in their destruction; by the troublous times which followed, compelling him to throw aside the reed and graver for the sword; by the crowd of stirring and mighty events which have since engrossed his labors, leaving him no leisure for meditations on antiquity; and, not least of all, by the painful and unattractive nature of the theme itself, involving so much of national disorder and humiliation? Now, however, that these buildings have been restored again to the light of day, with all their beautiful monuments and precious records; now that a long period of peace and prosperity is in store for the people; now that the grandeur and glory of the empire are so completely restored, and so vastly augmented that we can bear to hear patiently the story of past troubles—now is the season, indeed, of all others, for the historian to take up this subject, and worthily to treat it, ay, and gratefully to contrast the reverses and sufferings of those times with the splendors and happiness of to-day.

But I must answer your last question, namely, What are the king's intentions, in connection with these discoveries? This subject was discussed at length, in the course of an interview to which he was graciously pleased to summon me last evening, but no positive decision was arrived at. The temples will undoubtedly be restored according to the plans of their founder, with additional decorations and inscriptions; the tower, also, is to be erected forthwith, and will rise more majestic and beautiful than ever. It is to be embellished, without and within, with the choicest paintings and sculptures, and, ere long, we shall see the holy fires shedding their beneficent light from the altar that is to crown its summit. As to the palace itself, whether it is to be rebuilt after the original designs, whether a larger and more beautiful one is to occupy its place, whether, after duly removing its treasures and copying its inscriptions, the materials shall be employed in the construction of a palace immediately to the south of it, for prince Adrammelech, or, finally, whether no structure shall be erected over it, save a commemorative obelisk, in the middle of a pleasant garden, enlivened by fountains—all these various suggestions have been made and considered, but no one definitely adopted. His majesty was pleased to express himself at length, on all these points, and in his usual quick and energetic manner—we pacing meanwhile the eastern terrace of the palace, under the beautiful moonlight. After nearly two hours' conversation, I was summoned to partake of the royal supper, in one of the chambers of the northern court. The queen was present, and one of her little daughters, and likewise the Princes Sharezer and Essarhaddon. The queen was lovely and gracious as ever, and had much to say in commendation of the industry of the young princess, whose pretty little fingers were fast finishing a most exquisite piece of embroidered work. She also showed me some drawings and paintings of hers, which evinced abilities truly surprising for her years. Prince Sharezer was unusually taciturn and self-absorbed; but Prince Essarhaddon amused us greatly by his droll remarks and funny stories. He is a rare mimic. At his mother's request, he sang what he called his Bird-Song, in which he introduced very playfully and adroitly, the most perfect imitations of all the notes of all the fowls of the air, from the screams of the eagle, down to the finest trills of the nightingale; contrasting them in a very piquant manner, and connecting them by bits of verse of his own composition, which were full of pleasant satire, not unmixed with pathos. His father laughed heartily at some of his sallies. He is evidently a favorite of his, and, under all his apparent levity, hides a large heart, and great acuteness and activity of mind. His majesty retired shortly after supper, and also the Prince Sharezer. As I was about taking my leave, the young princess seized me by the robe, and insisted on my playing draughts with her. Of course, I had to obey, and the board was straightway produced; a present, it seems, which her father had made her that very day, and a most superb birthday gift, indeed. To say truth, my eyes were so bewitched with its splendors, and the exquisite carving and costume of the pieces, that I lost three games running, before I was aware of it, and to the unbounded delight of the fair conqueror. And, indeed, I should hardly have won the fourth, but for the manifest drowsiness of the princess. No wonder, poor child, after all the fatigues and excitements of the day. There had been a grand gathering of children at the palace, in the morning, in her honor, and a feast; previous to which, a magnificent bouquet had been presented to her, in behalf of the young damsels of Nineveh—each child presenting a single flower. The queen was so good as to show it to me, in an adjoining chamber—a cluster of gems, truly, and full of pretty meanings to those who know how to read this pleasant, mystic flower-language. But now, I have something to tell you, of a far less agreeable nature. As I was leaving the palace, and while turning an angle of one of the corridors of the north wing, I came suddenly upon the Prince Sharezer. He had a frightful scowl upon his face, his right hand grasped his dagger convulsively, and he was muttering some words to himself, which I could not make out, though they seemed to refer to some enemy close at hand. I would fain have avoided him, but it was too late. He started on seeing me, and for a moment looked as if he would willingly have plunged his weapon in my breast. He presently recovered himself, however, and, with a grave salutation, allowed me to pass on. I need not tell you how startled and pained I was at such an apparition. More than once, lately, I have detected, as I thought, a bad expression in the prince's countenance; as if he were brooding over some fancied injury, or cherishing some wicked ambition, or groundless jealousy —listening, in short, to some cursed suggestion of the evil one, whatever it might be. At other times, again, he has been so civil and affable, that I have dismissed my suspicions as the offspring of my own wicked imagination. But this strange encounter of last night sadly confirms them. What *can* it mean? What possible cause of offense can he have, and with whom? He, certainly, is not so much beloved as his brothers, either by the king or the people; still, he has the reputation of a brave and skillful soldier, and is by no means deficient in other accomplishments. Ah, I wish he were exhibiting his soldiership, this moment, in some distant corner of the empire. I have a strange foreboding that some mischief is at hand. Heavens, if any calamity should overtake the nation, or our good king; now, too, when we are at the very height of our happiness and renown—and by *such* means, too! But no, no, no, it cannot be: the thought is too monstrous to be harbored for a moment. It must have been some vision of my disordered fancy.

Such, my dear friend, was the burden of my thoughts, as I walked slowly homewards; and, indeed, it was long before I could recover my serenity—balmy as was the air, and lovely the night. On reaching my own house, I was surprised to find Zeresh still up, and evidently distressed about something. You must know that your little favorite, Semiramis, while frolicking in the garden, yesterday afternoon, with Rough, our venerable house-dog, was so unlucky as to run a thorn into her foot. Inflammation set in rapidly, and the poor thing lay awake all night, moaning with pain. The doctor called early this morning, and found her in a high fever. He promptly administered some cooling medicine, and says she must be kept perfectly quiet for the next two or three days.

On entering the palace this morning, my thoughts naturally reverted to the painful scene of last night. Almost the very first person I met, on entering the Archive Chamber, was Prince Sharezer himself. He stopped me, and was studiously civil and conversable. Not the slightest allusion, however, did he make to what had occurred, though he watched my countenance very narrowly all the time he was talking. I know not what to make of him. But I must not dwell again upon this disagreeable subject, and can only trust that my suspicions and misgivings are without foundation.

Several couriers have arrived to-day from all parts of the empire. Among the many dispatches that I read to his majesty, was a very pleasant letter from the king of Tyre, accompanying a gift of wine, which he says has been reposing quietly in his cellars for more than a century, and on the cordial qualities of which he dwells with great warmth of language. He also sends with the wine two beautiful golden vases, made of the gold from the newly discovered Spanish mines, the inexhaustibleness of which he is also very eloquent about, and the new impulse which they will give to the trade of the world. There was also a letter from King Miliddu-ris, announcing the safe arrival of his son, Minuas, full of thanks, and promises, and self-abasement, as usual. There were a few lines appended, from the young prince himself, the touching pathos and simplicity of which most happily contrasted with the verbosity of his weak-minded father; a man in whose truthfulness I have no faith whatever. Poor youth! I wish he were in the hands of better teachers, for he has all the elements of greatness in him. There was, likewise, a very tedious and pompous epistle from the king of Persia, to which his majesty listened with ill-suppressed impatience. It was not easy, indeed, to decipher the writer's meaning, so buried was it under a mass of tawdry rhetoric and affected phraseology. One passage, however, in which he darkly insinuates his suspicions as to the good faith of King Deioces, and ventures to suggest that it might be as well, perhaps, to keep a strict watch upon the movements of the Median ambassador, aroused the hearty indignation of his majesty. "This sweet-lips, this milk-sop, this nerve-shattered debauchee—what means he by his pitiful inuendoes against one of the wisest and best of princes? Is it to divert our attention from his own small villainies, that he asperses thus his betters? If he hath aught to say, why not say it in plain, downright Assyrian? But I will give him a lesson in letter-writing that he will remember." And thereupon the king dictated an epistle, the brief pungency of which certainly *ought*, at once, to mend the style and awake the fears of the unlucky prince whose folly had provoked it. Between ourselves, however, I cannot help thinking that his majesty is a little annoyed at the growing power and fame of the Median king, and that he will not altogether neglect the hints, even of this imbecile Persian.

After the audience, and the due entry of these transactions in the Palace Journal, I availed myself of an hour's leisure to explore the Phoenician chamber, which, you are aware, the artists were restoring and redecorating at the time you left us. Their labors are now concluded, and the effect is grand. The sculptures have been carefully retouched and recolored throughout; the inscriptions have been newly filled, and shine like gold; the paintings of the eastern and western walls have been obliterated, and their places supplied by far more beautiful and elaborate ones, and the ceiling has been raised several feet, and pierced with four new circular lights, while the whole character of its decorations has been changed. The carved work, mostly in cedar, of some of the compartments, is the most exquisite I ever beheld, and the borders of the new windows, in gold and ivory, are exceedingly rich. The old brick pavement has been replaced by a superb one of alabaster, appropriately inscribed. The raising of the ceiling is a great improvement, making the proportions of the room far more agreeable to the eye; still more so, the pouring in this flood of grateful light from the additional openings. True, the solemn effect of the holy images at the portals is somewhat impaired by it, but this defect is a hundred-fold compensated by its revealing the numberless minute beauties of the sculptures and paintings, that would otherwise have been lost. In a word, from having been rather a gloomy chamber, it is now one of the most splendid and cheerful in the palace. As I stood lingering over its many attractions, suddenly the superb purple curtain was drawn aside from the southern portal, and a picture was revealed, the magnificence of which no familiarity can ever make wearisome. The spacious platform, with its noble pavement, the scattered guards in shining armor, the slender pillars, with their gay streamers caressed by the gentle breeze, the stately staircase, lined with couchant lions, and below, the blended domes, villas, gardens, towers, fortresses, obelisks, the Tigris, with its marble bridges, its huge rafts and barges, its numberless vessels with their many-colored sails, receding in the distance, as they were borne along its silver windings, the snow-white clouds above, slow sailing through the deep blue sky, all these things combined to form a scene, which surely no other on earth can parallel.

On my way home from the palace, this afternoon, I met our dyspeptic, hypochondriacal friend, Malech. Poor fellow, he has a pretty hard time of it. He has fallen away terribly, walks with great feebleness, and is troubled, also, with a violent and oft-recurring cough. In addition to this, several of his most important and valuable teeth have, as he expressed it, deserted their posts in time of action, and thus by no means increased the beauty or cheerfulness of his countenance, or the clearness of his articulation. And yet, with all these difficulties, his old habit of fast and loud talking, and of quaint phraseology, seems to cling to him. How I wish you could have heard his reply to my salutation, and the long catalogue of his sorrows and ailments that he recounted to me, as I gave him my arm for a square or two. Such a strange mixture of sweet, sour, bitter, sad, funny, sarcastic, grotesque, picturesque, I am sure never fell before from the lips of Assyrian. His wits are as bright as ever, and his fancy as full of imagery, but his powers of expression are, of course, greatly impaired, from the abovementioned causes. This struggle between mental activity and bodily debility produced an effect, at one moment, quite touching, and at another, exceedingly ludicrous. Especially, did some of those long words, that our friend is so fond of employing, task and perplex him. In the midst of a convulsive effort to bring forth one of these octosyllabic monsters, there came a sudden and most unmannerly puff of wind, which, absurd to relate, seized upon Malech's ill-secured wig, and bearing it through the air in triumph, caused it finally to alight in a pool of water, some fifty yards distant, leaving its late wearer in a truly piteous condition. In vain, however, did I attempt to assume an expression of respectful sympathy. Nature would have her wicked way, and a fit of immoderate laughter was the consequence, in which the poor invalid himself, after a feeble and plaintive remonstrance, finally joined with evident relish, till his returning cough presently recalled him to a sense of his wretchedness. Meanwhile, the fat slave in attendance experienced no little difficulty in recovering the fugitive wig. He returned with it at last, however, much exhausted by his efforts, making, moreover, the most diabolical faces, in his ineffectual attempts to preserve his gravity. Poor Melech, I was right glad when he was safely deposited again within his own doors. Unless a favorable change soon takes place in him, his walks and talks are numbered. Do not think me heartless in making fun thus, of the poor sufferer, for really, the quaint and absurd way in which he gives vent to his feelings is irresistibly ludicrous. He longs to be off, he says, and to be snugly ensconced in his alabaster residence; out of the reach of scolding women, and thieving slaves, and lying quacks, and clamorous duns. (Our dear friend will leave but little gold dust behind him, I fear.) *Little house, great comfort;* he is only waiting, he says, to have these words sculptured on his coffin before taking possession, and he hopes the marigolds will be blowing, and the palms waving over him, long before this time next year. It certainly looks as if his wishes would be gratified. Poor fellow! what to him, indeed, are all the splendors of

Nineveh; all the glories of the empire? What brightness in the skies, what beauty in the fields, *can* there be to the wretched bond-slave of dyspepsia? For years, now, has our dear friend been groaning under this cruel tyranny, and ought we to blame him for expressing himself warmly, or for sighing for his freedom? Had he committed any excesses that would seem to explain and justify these sufferings, it would be different; but for a man of his impulsive temperament, and lively imagination, his life has been a remarkably calm and temperate one. Well, well, we must leave him in the hands of the good gods, who have their own wise ends in view, no doubt, in trying him thus, though our imperfect understandings cannot decipher them. He will soon be released now, soon solve the problem of destiny, and I believe happily, and that the annoyances and sufferings of his closing years on earth will but the more enhance those joys and glories that are in store for him, amid the never-fading bowers of Elysium.

On reaching home, I was delighted to find that our dear little child was much better, with hardly any fever about her. She is now sleeping quietly, and will be herself again in a day or two. We had a very pleasant call this evening from Zethar, who had a great deal to say about you, and, as usual, chanted your praises with great fervor. But it is past midnight, and my letter is quite long enough already. Some passages in it you will, of course, see the propriety of keeping to yourself. And so, my dear friend, farewell. The gods ever bless and keep you.

TELASSAR.

LETTER VIII.

MEMUCAN TO TELASSAR.

Many thanks, my dear friend, for your numerous and pleasant letters. You have, indeed, been as much better than your word, in this regard, as I have fallen behind mine. And, to say truth, I take up my reed to-day, more at the bidding of an accusing conscience than because I have anything of interest to tell you.

Our new palace progresses very, very slowly. It is more than four months now, since our arrival here, and, save in the way of demolition, faint, indeed, are the traces of our labors. This is not owing to any want of zeal on the part of his majesty, or to any lack of laborers, or materials; but simply because the plans themselves, when we come to realize them, are so much more vast and difficult, and costly than was expected. Ah, dear, I suppose it always *will* be so; what looks so fair and inviting, when traced on papyrus, or moulded in the miniature clay-model, must needs become a formidable, and, too often, a soul-vexing task, ere it is finally embodied in the massive and lasting marble. My twelvemonth here, I foresee clearly, will result in a four years' residence, at least. And yet, I would not be thought to complain, save for the separation from dear friends at Nineveh. On the contrary, I have every reason to be grateful for having found such a prince for an employer—so liberal in his payments, so uniformly gracious and condescending in his manners, and, moreover, so intelligent on all subjects of art. He has many just, many beautiful ideas concerning it and its high calling; not tamely adopted from others, but evidently the fruit of his own reflections; some of them, indeed, quite original. It is truly delightful at times to see the graceful way in which he throws aside the splendors and majesty of his station and becomes simply the courteous and genial man—one, who not only speaks freely and playfully himself, but encourages the same freedom in others—one, indeed, of the few autocrats of earth who prefers to rule by love and not by fear.

I have many other good friends here also, and agreeable acquaintances. There is abundance of excellent society in the city—a great deal to see, and learn, and enjoy. As I have said before, life has not that same air of dignity and repose here which it wears at home. There is far more of impulse and of tumult, both in the employments and amusements of the people, than I have been accustomed to; certainly more grossness of manners in the lower classes—a thing inevitable in such a place of rendezvous of the men of all lands. On the other hand, there is a ceaseless variety of persons and of objects, which far better repays the observations of the student of life. The artist, too, what an inexhaustible gallery of subjects he has before him—what strange, and ever-shifting combinations of forms, and colors, and costumes. The student of languages, also, has advantages here nowhere else to be found on earth. All their different structures, affinities, and antipathies may here be explored, and reduced to first principles. There is not an important dialect of any known tongue but what may be studied here in all its phases and modifications—as it is heard from the lips of ambassadors in solemn addresses to the throne, or in the conversation of distinguished strangers, or in the quaint ballads and marvelous tales of foreign story-tellers and wandering minstrels, or, again, in the familiar speech and tavern-altercations of foreign traders and mariners, or, finally, in the gibberish of the market-places. I repeat it, this is the spot of all others on earth, where the materials may be found for that which, if scientifically constructed, would be a priceless treasure to the scholar—a universal and philosophic grammar. I had the honor of conversing with his majesty recently, on this very point, and I have reason to believe that, among the many noble ideas and enterprises which interest his mind, this one will not be overlooked.

And then, the markets of Babylon; who can ever think of them without boundless wonder and delight? Such congregations of merchants, such infinite treasures, spoils of all seas and shores, products of the industry of all nations! What possible wish of the heart, what whim of luxury, cannot here be gratified? Is it food that the purchaser seeks? What a table is here spread for him, embracing the grains, fruits, herbs, the fish, flesh, fowl of all regions, from the rice of Taprobana to the barley of Thracia—from the wild boar of Scythia to the potted hare of Abyssinia. Or drink? What cannot the customer get for his gold-dust, from the cheap cider of Accad or the bitter beer of Dura, to the fragrant cordials of Susa, the far-brought and luscious Mendesian, or the sparkling, exhilarating Chian? Or clothing? Who shall presume to set forth its infinite varieties, from the goodly garment of the noble, with its golden devices on a purple ground, or embroidered all over with gay pictures or sacred legends, down to the coarse, harsh sack-cloth tunic of the galley-slave? Or horses? Here they are, Parthian, Assyrian, Arabian, of all shades of color and degrees of fleetness—those that exult in the battle, and those that prance in gay attire in the pageants of princes. Or oxen, or sheep, or goats? What noble flocks and herds are here, alike those that are destined for the peaceful labors of the field, and those that are set apart for the service of the gods. Or camels, or dromedaries? Where else will you find such droves to pick from, alike those that jog steadily along beneath their heavy burdens, and those that fly over the plains, like the wind, bearing the decrees of monarchs? Or monkeys? Here are the wretches, of all sizes and prices—a vast and various family, of every style of ugliness, but all alike nasty, mischievous, and intelligent. Or seek you a dog, whether for the chase, or to protect your house, or to amuse its inmates? You need not be long in finding your object in this great gathering—be it the little, waddling, peevish, cream-fed lap-dog of Thebes, or the huge, noble-fronted, iron-limbed mastiff of India. Or are you in quest of spices, or incense, or perfumes, or poisons, or precious woods or stones? In what other port of earth will you find them in such profusion and variety, from the huge sacks and bottles filled with Arabian gums, down to the tiny phial, in whose little cell are stored the virtues of ten thousand flowers, or the terrors of some hell-brewed liquid, in whose every drop resides the annihilating force of the thunderbolt; from the thin strip of alabaster, on which our children draw their quaint devices, or achieve their little victories in arithmetic, to the vast column that is to grace the heart of some stately city, and to tell distant ages of the exploits of some mighty conqueror? But why dwell on these things, or enumerate them to you, who are already so familiar with them? Why speak of this constant din and murmur of traffickers, these ever-shifting groups, these infinitely varied expressions, the sleek and the hunger-pinched, the crafty and simple, the proud and the abject—these strangely blended costumes, and complexions, and dialects? Or of the vast stores of knowledge that may be gathered here, both of the works of the gods, and of the useful or perverse inventions of their children? I regret that I have not more leisure to enjoy and study them as I would. Zethar seems to take great delight in resorting to them, and daily brings home some interesting story that he has heard, or droll encounter that he has had. With all his social tastes, however, and roving propensities, I must do him the justice to say, that he is much more of a student than he was. He is losing his disrelish for scientific investigations, and is already a good geometer and skillful draughtsman. In truth, he has given evidence of excellent parts, and, if he will but persevere, I doubt not that he will, some day, quite outshine his father, as an architect.

The city has been even livelier than usual for the last few days. This is owing partly to the presence of Prince Ardys, son of the good King Gyges, of Lydia, who has been making us a visit, and has been most warmly welcomed by his majesty. The news of his arrival here has, no doubt, reached Nineveh ere this. He has been spending some months in Egypt, has also visited the principal cities of Syria and Phœnicia, and is last from Jerusalem. You will soon have the pleasure of seeing him at the metropolis, whence he goes to Palmyra, and so home, by the way of Tarsus. He will then have completed a grand tour, undertaken at the command of his royal father, who, as you know, is beginning to feel the infirmities of age, and who wished his son to see somewhat of the world before assuming, as in the order of nature he soon must, the cares and duties of sovereignty. Such, at least, is the avowed motive of the good king; though it would appear from secret dispatches to his majesty, that his real object is to dissipate, if possible, the melancholy which has overtaken the prince since that unhappy quarrel, so fatal to both, between his two elder brothers, to the younger of whom he was most tenderly attached. I have had the honor of being presented to him, and was greatly pleased with his appearance and conversation. He has evidently derived much benefit from his travels. Once or twice, indeed, I noticed that his mind wandered a little, his handsome face became suddenly clouded, and the sentence died unfinished on his lips; but he soon recovered himself, and when released from these sad memories, his conversation was full of intelligence and sprightliness; a prince, certainly, of more natural gifts than his father, whose reign, thus far, has been by no means so illustrious or eventful as its strange and romantic beginning seemed to promise. Under these circumstances, his majesty has, of course, taken unusual pains to make his visit agreeable to his guest: regattas, hunts, hawking-parties, banquets, have all been had in his honor; and one evening an illumination of the principal buildings of the city, which was exceedingly beautiful—its most conspicuous feature being the observatory, with its admirably defined pillars and arches—the summit being crowned with a huge sphere, composed of myriads of many-colored lights, the magnificent appearance of which, and of its image as reflected in the river, I leave you to fancy.

We had a grand hawking-party the other day, which his majesty graciously invited me to join. The scene of our sport was the beautiful plain immediately to the west of the lake and grove of Hira, on the edge of which his majesty has a charming little hunting lodge, recently erected. You are, doubtless, familiar with the place; about ten parasangs to the south of the city, and a most delightful ride all the way. We were three days absent—a company of about sixty, including the attendants—all well mounted, with a noble pack of hounds, who greatly distinguished themselves, and a most select company of falcons. Conspicuous among them, was the royal favorite, Adon, that renowned bird, whose exploits have been the theme of more than one minstrel of the court. He sat in state, perched upon the wrist of his master, with all his finery on, and seemed to be fully conscious of his high position and well-merited fame. His hood was richly wrought, and gay with tassels, the eyes being formed of precious stones. His jesses were of rare workmanship, and he had golden bells upon his legs. When the hood was removed, I did not fail to pay him the tribute of my homage. Though already in his fourteenth summer, and the hero of so many fights, his eye is as piercing as ever, his talons as sharp, his flight as swift, his stroke as fatal. Woe betide the poor partridge or bustard, hare or gazelle, at whom those wicked, far-seeing orbs are leveled. Nay, he will not hesitate to attack the imperial eagle himself, and more than once has narrowly escaped tasting death, in his rash onslaughts. It was quite late at night before we reached the lodge, and at daybreak our sports commenced. Though not participating in them so actively as some of my companions, I was, nevertheless, exceedingly delighted. It was a charming morning, with a gentle breeze stirring the leaves, and a few clouds scattered over the sky, enough to temper the brilliant rays of the sun. The elastic turf, the sparkling dew-drops, the gorgeous flowers, that dotted the plain, the exhilarating movements of our horses, the cheering cries of the huntsmen, the beautiful groups that were constantly forming and dispersing, the marvelous displays of courage and sagacity, on the part both of dogs and birds, all combined to form a scene, whose delicious excitement the saddest heart could not resist. Our guest enjoyed it vastly, and was uniformly among the first to come up with the quarry. We flew our birds at whatever offered, not neglecting the waterfowl, who are attracted hither by the neighboring lake. A light car with two horses followed us, to secure the spoils, and its rich and varied contents bore witness to the success of our labors. Among them were geese, ducks, hares, bustards, partridges, innumerable, a few cranes, and, to crown our triumph, no less than half a dozen gazelles. This part of the sport was, indeed, most beautiful and exciting. Scorning any less noble game, Adon reserved his powers for these victims; and, truly, he justified his fame and lineage. Three times did I witness his performances; saw him fix his fatal eye upon the doomed one, separate him from his companions, dart at him like an arrow, arrest him bounding in mid-air, pin his head to the ground, twice repeat the blow, the second time looking up with fluttering wing, impatient for the advent of the hound, his chosen partner in the work of death; and when the dog (a noble creature, worthy of such a bird) came up with the victim, returning, uncalled, to meet his master, with a hoarse note, expressive of ill-suppressed delight, and a look of triumph in his burning eye. Right heartily did I join in the applauses bestowed upon him, and, had I been a poet, should certainly have indited a ballad in his honor. The other falcons, too, acquitted themselves right handsomely; one, especially, a much larger bird than Adon, with superb speckled plumage, who, while in pursuit of a crane, was pounced upon by two ruffianly kites at the same moment. With wonderful address and swiftness did he at first elude, and, in turn, attack his assailants, punishing one with instant death, by a most happily administered blow, which caused him to drop like a stone to the earth, and finally killing the other, after a severe struggle on the ground, coming out of the fight himself uninjured, though sadly shorn of his beautiful feathers. The sun was nearly five hours high when we gave up the chase, and returned to the lodge with our spoils. Here a welcome repast awaited us, which we attacked without ceremony, and with well-earned appetites. Afterwards his majesty retired to his study, it being an inflexible rule of his, to devote two hours of each day to meditation and reading, if possible, whether in camp or in palace, in health or in sickness. The young prince did me the honor to invite me to play at draughts with him, while the rest of our company dispersed, some to sleep, others to sail on the lake, or to recline in the cool bowers of the beautiful garden attached to the lodge. We assembled again in the evening, at a superb supper, in which the royal cooks achieved wonders. Then came music, both with voice and harp. That glorious old ballad in honor of the chase, the composition of our divine Ninus, was finely sung, his majesty himself joining in the chorus. We had much pleasant story-telling likewise—our guest relating many agreeable anecdotes concerinng his travels in Egypt, and his adventures at the court of King Sabaco. He repeated, also, several witty sayings of that most jovial of monarchs, the good king of Tyre. It was still early when we retired to rest, and at dawn our sports were resumed. They were not prolonged to the same degree, however, as on the day previous—his majesty being compelled to return to the city that same evening. It was almost midnight, indeed, of the third day, when we reëntered the gates, after a lovely ride—a beautiful full moon having been our torch-bearer.

But I have this moment received a summons to attend his majesty, and must e'en leave Zethar to finish this epistle. Ever thine, MEMUCAN.

* * * * *

I have duly sharpened my reed, dear kinsman, in obedience to the above command, and proceed, however unworthily, to fill up the remainder of this roll. And first, need I assure you how anxious I am to see you all again, to look upon the sweet face of dear aunt Zeresh, and to hear the pleasant prattle of the children? Or how grieved I am, that it will be so long before I can enjoy these privileges? Our stay here, as father says, will probably be much nearer five years than one. No doubt, however, the king, ever kind and gracious, will grant us an occasional leave of absence, of which how joyfully shall we avail ourselves! As to your ever paying us a visit, that, I know, is quite out of the question; your duties are altogether too constant and arduous to admit of it. But I don't see why you could not send Hegai to us, for a few months. (Be pleased, by the way, to give him a good scolding in my name, for not having taken the slightest notice of either of my last three letters.) He has evidently been studying too hard lately, and a little relaxation will do him good. We should both be delighted to see him.

You will be gratified to learn that I am becoming of some use to father, in his profession, and daily render him substantial service, both with reed and graver; that I am taking more and more interest continually in his beautiful art, and have finally made up my mind to adopt it as my calling. I am at last convinced that the gods never meant me for a soldier, but that I have talents as an artist (and father's criticisms encourage me in this conviction), which, properly developed, may yet do me honor, and the state some service. Father says that he has never yet been able to find the word *fail*, in *his* Assyrian lexicon, and, surely, with such an inspiring example before me, ought I not to take heart? Still, I have not yet become so persevering and thorough a student, but what I do occasionally (as he has above intimated) run away from my tools and manuscripts, in order to enjoy the manifold novelties, oddities, and curiosities of this wonderful city. I confess I take endless delight in exploring its streets and shops, its quays and vessels from all ports, in watching the motley throngs that crowd its temples, and in studying the infinite humors of its market-places. How like, and yet how strangely unlike our own Nineveh! Be not alarmed, dear kinsman, I shall not have the presumption to undertake any long-drawn parallel between the two capitals; especially after what father has written upon the subject, simply remarking that of all the cities of earth, this, I should think, must be the one where the student of human nature can learn his lessons to most advantage; those out-door lessons, not so arduous truly, and exacting as those of the closet—but none the less needful to true wisdom; the place where one would most readily lay aside his prejudices, abandon his dreams and theories, and look the naked facts of humanity full in the face, with all their lights, and all their shadows; the place to learn forbearance in, and toleration; where one feels more keenly and constantly than elsewhere, that, beneath all the infinite varieties of speech, creed, costume, complexion among men, the same human heart is ever beating; that we are all children alike of the same common ancestors—having the same relationship to the ever-blessed gods; ay, and the same sad kin-ship in guilt and misery; the same perverse preference of our own brutal appetites and blood-thirsty propensities to deeds of piety and love; the same—" Stop, stop, stop! Belus preserve us, what a long and solemn sentence! And this from the 'lips, too, of our thoughtless Zethar!' Why, what has come over the lad?"

Such, dear uncle, is your natural and just criticism on the above bundle of commonplaces. Most humbly do I ask pardon for presuming to sit, even for a moment, in the chair of the moralist, and straightway resume my native frivolity.

You must know that my town-studies have been materially aided of late, by a present from dear Adar. Among the innumerable evidences of his good-will, he gave me, the other day, a most charming dromedary—a perfect love of a creature, as white as snow, as fleet as the wind, as gentle as a lamb. A baby might manage him, so good-tempered is he, and he has the easiest trot imaginable.

His appointments, I need not tell you, were worthy of him—a beautifully decorated saddle, with a comfortable seat behind for a friend; a scarlet cloth with rich fringe and tassels; a dainty guide-stick, and a sweet-toned silver bell about his neck. I have ridden him several times, and have tried all his paces, and find them all alike pleasant. Indeed, I doubt if there be a more beautiful or serviceable beast in all Babylon; and I find myself quite the admiration and envy of the youngsters here, whenever I make my appearance on him in the streets. As the best evidence of his powers, he took me completely round the walls of the city yesterday, in less than ten hours, with perfect ease; stopping many times, too, to allow his rider to enjoy the beautiful picture around him. In old-fashioned times, you know, this used to be called a two-days' journey. After this feat, need I sing his praises further? Oh, how I wished little Zeresh had been with me!

While I think of it, let me tell you of a sight I saw in the streets, the other day; one of the drollest and most extraordinary, certainly, that I ever beheld; a procession of monkeys, bearing on their backs, hods of bricks and bitumen, ascending and descending the ladders in front of a building going up in our neighborhood, and, I assure you, performing their duties with all the ease, method, and decorum of human beings. They were all dressed alike, with their tails closely cropped, and were about the size of big boys. I stood more than an hour watching them, and was deeply impressed with the ability and faithfulness which they manifested; and this, notwithstanding occasional attempts, on the part of some mischievous urchins, to lead them into temptation, by artfully dropping nuts and cakes at the foot of the ladders. Once, indeed, a poor monkey's virtue gave way before the charms of a huge dough-nut, which few children could have resisted; but a smart application of the whip of the overseer promptly recalled him to his place in the line; the tempters themselves scampering down the street, as if Typho were after them. This was the only instance, however, of disobedience that occurred, while I was present. When the proper season for refreshment arrived (so remarked the overseer to me), it was beautiful to see the orderly way in which the creatures dropped their hods, and formed a social circle, while partaking of their noon-tide meal. I repeat it, I was wonderfully entertained and impressed by this strange exhibition. True, I had heard of something of the kind before—had heard cousin Menahem speak of the many accomplishments of some of the monkeys of India, and also of Abyssinia—of these last, especially, and their officiating occasionally as torch-bearers at supper-parties, and otherwise making themselves useful. I remembered, too, those queer old Egyptian pictures of yours, in which these creatures are represented as assisting the laborers in vintage-time, and also in the sycamore trees, handing down the figs to the gardeners; but I confess, I thought that, in the one case, our kinsman was merely uttering the inventions of his own lively fancy, and that, in the other, the artist was indulging his sense of humor, somewhat at the expense of truth. After what I have seen recently, however, I have no right to doubt their accuracy. Father, I notice, alludes, in his letter, to the monkey-market here, and to the intelligence of the beasts; but none of the filthy tricks I had witnessed in it, were at all calculated to prepare my mind for such a spectacle as that which I have just described. I spoke of it that same day to Adar, at supper, and asked him if it was possible that the demand for labor, in Babylon, so far exceeded the supply, that they were compelled to press these creatures into service thus? "Not at all," said he; "it is merely a wild freak of the owner of the property, a notorious humorist here, who has long been considered about three-quarters crazy. And yet, the signal success of his experiment seems rather to vindicate the soundness of his wits, while it also affords much matter for curious speculation, to the thoughtful mind." Our good friend then dwelt, at considerable length, on the many probable and possible latent virtues and undeveloped abilities of the world of animals around us, both sacred and profane; talking very pleasantly of the changes that might take place in the social system, were they properly educated, and illustrating his ideas by many interesting anecdotes of grateful dogs, affectionate horses, long-suffering dromedaries, thoughtful elephants, nay, even of filthy swine themselves, who had, on more than one occasion within his knowledge, given evidence of high intelligence, and of kindly feeling. I must not repeat any of these stories to you, though I found them exceedingly entertaining and instructive at the time. Dear me, it would take an acre of papyrus, were I to tell you a tenth part of the queer adventures I have had since I have been here—the droll creatures I have met, their quaint ideas, and modes of expression. True, I have been quite shocked and grieved at times, but far oftener exhilarated and instructed. There is undoubtedly much more freedom of speech and of manners here than at home, and a corresponding increase of eccentricity. Already is my sketch-book crowded with odd specimens from all the walks of life—from barbers up to generals, from pastry-cooks to high-priests; and though I should hardly venture to show it to you, I yet hope to have many hearty laughs over it with Hegai. The sailors here are an endless source of amusement to me. Too many of them are sad brutes, it is true, but others again are full of intelligence and vivacity, and especially those from Phœnicia.

The other day, I encountered an old Tyrian, who has followed the sea for threescore years and upwards, and yet his eye is as bright and his lungs are as sound as ever, and his bronzed and wrinkled face as cheerful as a boy's. Of course his Assyrian was not of the purest, but such as it was, he poured it forth with marvelous fluency and animation. His mind seemed to be a perfect storehouse of anecdotes, and as I sat on the deck of his old weather-stained vessel, he sang songs to me, and told stories about the terrors of the deep, and the wonders of far-off lands, with a blended humor and pathos, that many a pampered minstrel, or licensed jester of a court, might vainly strive to equal. His last voyage was from Taprobana, and, by his account, a fearfully tempestuous one. Will you believe it, at one time they were actually out of sight of land, for five consecutive days! Heavens and earth, five whole days, and not one glimpse of the friendly shore! Who would be a sailor? And yet the old fellow is evidently dying to be off again. His feet are burning under him, he says, and he can't sleep without rocking. I might tell you of others equally entertaining and instructive. I assure you, I have picked up an amount of geographical and commercial knowledge, in the course of my rambles along the quays here, that I would not willingly part with, and, above all, an insight into human nature—yes, more, I really believe, in three months' unrestrained intercourse here, than I should have done, in twice as many years, in our decorous, pompous Nineveh.

Father, I see, has told you all about our illustrious visitor, and of the entertainments in his honor—of the magnificent illumination, and of the hawking excursion which he enjoyed so greatly. One beautiful and curious sight, which we witnessed together the other day, he has not mentioned, however, namely, a miniature copy of Babylon done in wood, and colored, gilded, and decorated in precise imitation of the superb original. It is just finished, after many years' labor, and is the work of two brothers, both students in the college of Oannes, in one of the pleasant little gardens of which, we saw it under a glass house, built expressly to receive it. It is about forty feet square, exquisitely finished, and marvelously faithful. The walls, the brazen gates, the towers, temples, palaces, the park, river, bridges, shipping, the granaries, market-places, dock-yards, everything, in short, is here, just as in life—house for house, tree for tree, even down to the tiny threads of glass that represent the fountains in our own garden. And then the streets and squares, and markets, and quays, are filled with the very same groups of men and beasts that we daily meet in them. Nothing, indeed, seems wanting to complete the illusion, save the actual murmur of the great hive itself, and the clouds of smoke pouring forth from the tall chimneys of the factories. Such another monument of patient, faithful industry, I never expect to look upon again. Your mere utilitarian might object to it, perhaps, as an unprofitable employment of precious hours, better spent, forsooth, in money-getting; but, for myself, I confess I was charmed with it, and could have spent the whole day over it with delight. Father's searching eye detected a few small errors here and there, in the proportions, but, on the whole, he was very highly gratified, and warmly complimented one of the brothers, who was present, on the success of his labors.

But this is getting to be a pretty long voyage, and you, doubtless, think it high time for my vessel to come into port. You are quite right. I send you a parcel by this day's caravan, which I trust will arrive safely, and that its contents will prove acceptable. As you will perceive by the marks on the packages, the fans are a present from father to Aunt Zeresh, and were the very prettiest to be found in the city. The seal-ring is precisely in accordance with Hegai's instructions, and the device is the work of one of the most famous lapidaries here. If he is not satisfied with it, he must be hard to please, indeed. The pictured cloak is a love-token from father to dear Semiramis, as is the sandal-wood draught-board from her cousin. We have not forgotten little Zeresh, you will perceive, or the baby. The cane I hope you will like. The body of it, you will observe, is composed of many different kinds of wood, ingeniously put together, and you will not, I trust, consider the device on the top inappropriate to your calling, or time of life. Would that it were handsomer, but, to say truth, it is far from being high-water in my money-bags, at present. Ah, dear; the temptations to buy here are innumerable, and one's shekels are scattered and his gold-dust flying in all directions before he knows it.

And now, dear uncle, farewell for to-night. With best love to your household, whose pleasant faces I yet hope to see ere long, believe me your ever dutiful nephew, ZETHAR.

LETTER IX.

TELASSAR TO MEMUCAN.

We are quite disappointed, my dear friend, in being so long without a letter from you. You are not sick, surely, else would some mention have been made of it in Adar's charming letter, which we received yesterday. Do write soon, I beseech of you; or if your hours are, indeed, thus preoccupied, let us, at least, have a few lines from Zethar. There is nothing very interesting to tell you. We are all well at home. Your little namesake is coming on finely. Though hardly five months old yet, he already manifests great activity and perseverance as a creeper. His appetite, his mother says, is uniformly excellent, while I can bear witness to the soundness of his lungs. From what little I have seen of him, I should say that he was rather disposed to take hilarious views of life, than otherwise. Semiramis has quite recovered, and puts her pretty foot to the ground with her wonted decision. She resumed her studies some days since, and likewise the education of her flowers. She has received some choice seeds lately from Memphis, from our young friend, Akbar, which he has taken great pains to collect for her. They have been duly planted, and she is looking forward to a brilliant display in the spring. Akbar's last epistle, by the way, was a very entertaining one. In it he gives a long account of the funeral rites in honor of the sacred bull recently deceased, and of the pompous ceremonies attending the installation of his successor, which spectacles were, of course, entirely new to him, and the magnificence of which, he has portrayed with great animation.

Did I tell you that we had been enlarging our garden lately, to make up for the space occupied by the addition to the house? This last is in every way satisfactory. Our new banqueting chamber is very much admired, both for its proportions and decorations, and the lovely view from its western windows; and as for my new study, I am charmed with it, so quiet and cheerful, with such a soft light, and, above all, its exquisite ceiling. Thanks to that inventive brain of yours, so fertile in beautiful ideas. It is, indeed, all that priest or poet's heart could wish, and I can only regret that I have so few hours to spend in it.

Our family tomb, too, is at length completed. Here, I have ventured to deviate somewhat from your plans. Admirable as they are, I found them, on the whole, too sombre in their character. I confess, I do not see the propriety of making death and its surroundings so gloomy and forbidding, as we are too apt to do in Assyria. Why should not the last house be a cheerful one—its chambers enlivened with fair images, and the paths that lead to it adorned with flowers? Why should not the music of birds and of falling waters be near it, nay, everything that can attract, and soothe, and invite the mind to gentle meditation? I must say, this seems to me the great defect in our national character, this unwillingness to dwell on the thought of death, or if we do, this almost universal tendency to clothe it with attributes, at once grotesque and terrible—attributes which there is surely nothing in our holy religion to suggest or justify. Too many of us, alas, seem quite content to bask in the sunshine of to-day: so we may enjoy the brilliant spectacle, the sensual delights of the passing hour, we have nor word nor thought for the scenes beyond the grave. Hence is it that our funeral rites are so cold and unimpressive (how different herein from the other parts of our blessed ritual); that both priests and mourners are so impatient and restless under them, and that our places of sepulture are so unadorned, nay, repulsive, and so soon abandoned to decay and ruin. There are glorious exceptions, I know, scattered over the empire; still it is a national trait with which we are justly taxed by strangers. Herein, I confess I have much more sympathy with the men of Egypt than with my own countrymen. I love the social way in which their dead are brought together, the pleasant adornments of their tombs, the scenes of busy life that are portrayed in them, and their striking representations of the world to come—its rewards and punishments, its amenities and terrors. True, their treatment of these subjects is not always acceptable. There is occasionally a spirit of levity, and a proneness to caricature, which does not spare even the most sacred themes; but, in the main, they are dignified and impressive, and, at times, full of beauty. How different all this from our own naked, weather-stained, weed-encumbered monuments! I have often wished that we had a Necropolis, worthy of the name, in our magnificent Nineveh. What an addition it would be to its attractions, what a retreat for the priest and the student, what a new field it would open to our artists; but, above all, what refining and wholesome influences might it exert upon the minds of the people! Indeed, they sadly need them. If, as I said before, the funeral rites, even of our bravest and noblest, are but feebly and coldly performed, need I remind you of the scandalous neglect with which our dead poor are consigned to their final resting-place? Hurried, too often, into half-made graves, clad in unseemly garments, a brief prayer hastily mumbled over them, without a tear or flower to bear witness for them, without a stone or stake even, to indicate the spot where they lie. Is it not a strange anomaly, that a people so refined, so civilized, so scrupulously observant of the ceremonies of their religion in all other respects, should yet, in this regard, so sadly neglect its injunctions? Ay, and the priesthood themselves, with due deference be it spoken, are quite as blameworthy as those unto whom they minister. Truly, the heart of the nation needs to be stirred up on this subject. It is most humiliating to think how little of the intellect and art of the land is employed in expounding and illustrating the sublime doctrine of immortality—the very humblest and least enlightened of the nations that pay us tribute, herein surpassing ourselves, the world's proud masters. I have made bold, once or twice lately, encouraged by the kindness of his majesty, to speak at some length to him on this subject. He was pleased to express his approbation of what I said; he admitted that it was a great blot on the fair fame of Assyria, this neglect of our duties to the dead, and our unworthy views of the future life ; and thought it quite time to inaugurate a much-needed reform in these respects, which would at once elevate the sentiments of the people, and enlarge the boundaries of art. Indeed, from what he said, I could not help deriving the hope that, if the gods prolong his days, and confirm the prosperity of his empire, he will bring about some glorious changes in our social and religious life, and, moreover, leave behind him, in the shape of a magnificent cemetery, another of the myriad evidences of his piety and his zeal for the welfare of Assyria. The gods grant it, and may you, my dear friend, be chosen as the architect, to give fit expression to so noble a thought.

Pardon this long digression. I merely intended, at first, to apologize to you for presuming to deviate from your designs for our family resting-place ; but my poor reed has a perverse habit of wandering at times, as you know to your cost. But what changes have I been making ? Simply these : in the first place, I have altered the site of the monument, erecting it in the southwest corner of the garden, as being the most cheery and sunshiny spot in it. Secondly, I have enlarged the dimensions of the upper chamber, enlivening it at the same time with a gay pavement of many-colored tiles. Thirdly, I have removed those grim monsters that guarded the portal, and substituted therefor four beautiful figures in marble, illustrative of the seasons—the same that you liked so well, and the work of young Aphek, Hathan's favorite pupil. Finally, I have had the walls of the chamber covered with paintings and sculptures, as well as the arched ceiling—portraits of myself and Zeresh, our parents, and children, blended with rural scenes, and copies of the most beautiful buildings and views in the metropolis, all in medallions, tastefully arranged, and decorated with borders of various patterns: the whole being the work of the brothers Madon, and reflecting, I think, great credit on their genius. In a word, I have endeavored to make the place as attractive and suggestive as possible; so that, if our descendants, a century or two hence, see fit to come hither and muse over their dead-and-gone grandsires, they may associate them with cheerful images, and be tempted to linger here, and chat pleasantly over the past, and the changes time will have wrought in the mighty city. You may, perhaps, think this rather too bold an innovation; and, indeed, the design has been pretty sharply criticised in certain quarters; still, those whom I love best, and whose good voices I value most, speak approvingly of it. Zeresh is delighted, and has more than once, already, sought its welcome shade, taking her embroidery with her. All that is wanting, she says, is a sweet little fountain hard by, to which to attune one's fancies. But to return to the living.

I had a very pleasant excursion with Archilochus, yesterday, to the palace of King Sargon. We started early, and spent a large part of the day there, exploring its treasures, and wandering about its beautiful gardens. Our friend was in a very genial mood, and seemed to enjoy everything, from the beautiful gate of entrance, to the palace-roof itself. It was three months since my last visit, and never, indeed, did the place appear to me so charming, and in such perfect order. The stately terraces, with their dainty pavilions, gay flower-beds, and balustrades crowned with statues and vases, the noble flights of steps that connect them, the fish-ponds, the conservatory, the vast orangery, the lovely southern front of the palace, as seen through that glorious avenue of elms, the fountain, the obelisks—each of these things in turn, called forth the enthusiastic admiration of Archilochus; but above all, the magnificent panorama from the summit. He had ten thousand questions to ask—ten thousand brilliant things to say about it. I only wish he would embody some of them in one of those glorious odes of his. If ever there was a picture on earth to inspire the poet, surely this is the one. Nor did I fail to show our friend the manifold beauties and marvels of the interior—the superb Tyrian chamber; the famous water-organ, whose soft music quite charmed him; the cabinet of bronzes; the gift-chamber; the oratory, with its exquisite carved work; the study, with all its maps and models undisturbed, where our good king planned so many glorious enterprises, both of peace and war; and the chamber in which he breathed his last. The magnificent collection of butterflies, from all lands, appeared to have a peculiar fascination for our poet, and called forth many quaint and fanciful remarks from him. "Ah," said he, "if these brilliant creatures could but revive again, and fly forth together on a grand holiday-excursion, what a stir there would be among the youngsters of Nineveh! Or, if they were suddenly endowed with speech and reason, and were to tell, each in turn, his little tale, to the gorgeous crowd about him, would it not be the most various, and animated, and sparkling of histories?" In this pleasant vein did he moralize upon every object that he saw, his conversation being singularly free from those bitter, stinging remarks that, at times, disfigure it.

As we were passing through the orangery, we met the Prince Adrammelech. He was quite unattended, and seemingly lost in thought. His countenance did not wear its usual look of health and cheerfulness; something unpleasant was evidently disturbing him. He was very gracious, however, and addressed several kind words both to Archilochus and myself.

We returned home by the upper road, stopping for an hour or two at the house of Menahem. He was not at home, but we were hospitably received by his wife, who spread before us a repast which was quite acceptable after the labors of the morning. We had hardly finished it when the master made his appearance, accompanied by his little son and namesake, on a white pony—this being, his mother told us, his third appearance as a horseman —a bright child of some eight years, who certainly managed his steed with creditable skill and courage. Menahem was very cordial, and forthwith produced a flask of that famous wine of Calah, about which, you remember, he is so eloquent. He talked louder and faster than ever, flying from topic to topic in his usual desultory way, to the great amusement of Archilochus, and the evident mortification of his poor wife. After setting forth the praises of the wine, he proceeded to speak of agriculture in general—then of the proper rotation of crops—then he grew very warm about the absurdly high prices of beef and millet—next he regretted, with great earnestness, that some very valuable ideas of his, on the subject of irrigation, were so completely thrown away on the stupid farmers of the neighborhood; suddenly he took up the theme of piggeries, their proper dimensions and mode of construction, concluding his discourse with an invitation to us to come and see some mammoth swine of Persian extraction, of which he said he was very proud. In vain did we plead fatigue—drag us he would, all over his farm and gardens, hardly letting a rose-bush or a peach-tree pass without an eulogy. Among other things, he has been erecting in his garden a very fanciful dial, copied after one which he saw in Damascus, when on his travels; it is certainly a most ingenious and complicated contrivance, indicating not only the hours but the equinoxes and solstices, and other curious particulars. The shadow would have completely crossed it, had we waited to hear all its virtues rehearsed by our host. Poor Menahem, his infirmity is daily growing worse, and to say truth, we were very glad to run away from him.

Archilochus supped with us in the evening, Zothar being also present. We had much pleasant conversation, and mainly on topics of art. Zothar contended, with much earnestness, and at times, I thought, with more zeal than judgment, that we had already reached the acme of perfection, and that all future efforts of our own or other nations, whether in painting, sculpture or architecture, could be but mere imitations, more or less worthy, of the masterpieces of to-day; a proposition which Archilochus most warmly contested.

"I admit fully," said he, "the superb achievements of your artists, and in every department of art; nor, indeed, can I conceive of a picture more grand and gorgeous than that which I beheld yesterday evening, from the lovely hill of palms, on the opposite side of the river—namely, the magnificent palace of your king—illuminated by the setting sun, and mirrored in the majestic stream, with its graceful columns, its rich curtains of gold and purple, its cornices adorned with blended flowers and animals, its airy battlements, its portals guarded by divinities and enriched with sacred emblems, its shining inscriptions, its storied groups, commemorative of glorious victories; and then the neighboring stately temple, crowded with holy images, the vast platform itself, with its many-hued pavement, its spacious staircases, its standards gay with streamers, its scattered statues and obelisks, its groups of nobles, and priests, and soldiers. Cold and senseless, indeed, must be the man who could gaze without rapture on such a vision of beauty: and yet, when I approach this sumptuous palace more nearly, and faithfully peruse its sculptures, whether those that encrust its exterior or those that line its stately chambers, exquisitely finished and harmoniously colored as they are, yet how many graces and virtues in art are there which I do not find in them, or at best but feebly developed. How stiff are they—how monotonous, how crowded with conventionalisms—what errors of drawing, what sins against proportion and perspective, what dreary uniformity of expression! So far from recognizing in them that consummation of perfection which Zothar sees, they fall far, far indeed behind my ideal of excellence—not that I find that ideal better embodied elsewhere, or that these are not the best specimens of art the world has yet seen; at the same time, I believe that there are others in store, and that a very few centuries will reveal them to mortals, compared with which, these will seem the mere labors of school-boys. I speak frankly, friends, perhaps too boldly: nor, let me add, will Assyria be the scene where these high attributes of art are to be developed; ah! no, your artists ever have been, ever must be, quite too obedient to customs, and precedents, and the dicta of priests, too reverently submissive to the decrees of autocrats, to enjoy that freedom of thought and of expression essential to such development. To Greece, to my own dear land, is it reserved to achieve these triumphs; yes, I see it as clearly as if I were face to face to-day with their mighty works; I see the causes in operation that are to produce them—the nascent germs that are to ripen at last into temples, and palaces, and statues, and pictures—whose grace, beauty, majesty, infinite variety, are to fire the coming ages with enthusiasm, and to be memorable through all time."

I have described to you in previous letters the ardor of our friend, when he fairly dons his robe of prophecy, and paints the intellectual and artistic future of his country. He was quite as eloquent last night as on previous occasions, though the above is, of course, but a very meagre sketch of his remarks, which were poured forth with his usual rapidity and profusion of imagery. I do not presume to affirm or deny the justness of his views, or the probability of his predictions; he certainly said some things which I thought more showy than sound, and while expatiating upon the benefits of freedom to art and letters, quite too much overlooked its attendant dangers, more especially to that faith which it is their highest office to illustrate—dangers already sadly exemplified, according to his own statements, in the unworthy and gross conceptions of the majority of his countrymen, as to the nature and attributes of the blessed gods. But differ from, or agree with Archilochus as you may, who can help being fascinated by his ardent manner, his musical voice, his felicitous illustrations? Even Zothar, though quite puzzled and discomfited at times, seemed to be in no haste to break off the conversation, which was protracted to a late hour of the night.

I have been quite busy to-day at the palace, drafting several decrees, looking over numerous returns from the provinces, and adding up I know not how many formidable columns of figures. On my way to the audience-chamber this morning, I saw a magnificent chariot, which His Majesty has presented to our General, as a token of his approbation of his conduct in the Armenian campaign—and also a sword for young Meres, the exquisite embellishments and flattering inscriptions of which, I trust, will not turn the poor youth's head.

You will be glad to hear that the palace of Sardanapalus has, at last, been thoroughly explored, the only remaining chamber having been brought to light yesterday. Though itself plain and small, it yet contained many things of value and interest—among them some beautiful bronze ornaments, some very quaint ivory carvings, and numerous old tablets and cylinders, many of them of very great antiquity. These last have been duly deposited in the archive chamber. I have only had time to glance at one or two of the tablets, but saw enough to arouse my curiosity, referring as they did to our relations with Egypt nearly nine centuries ago. I shall not fail to give them a faithful examination, at my earliest leisure, and will report to you accordingly.

Since writing the above I have found a tenant for your house, in the person of Elath, a thriving merchant here, and a friend of Zothar, who gives him an excellent character: he expects to take possession in about ten days. I have also consummated the purchase of the strip of land adjoining, which you were so anxious to secure, and at a price so near that named by you, that I am sure you will not find fault with it. The deed has been delivered to me, and I shall send it to you to-morrow by special messenger. I have examined it carefully, and find it perfectly correct, with all the covenants, and the descriptions very minute and faithful. You will notice one peculiarity about it, namely, that there are only fifteen witnesses to each signature, instead of the usual twenty—a recent decree of the king having declared that number sufficient to give validity to all conveyances. It will indeed be a charming addition to your property, and I am only sorry that it will be so long before you will be here to improve and enjoy it.

On returning home this evening, by way of the old flower-market, I was greatly shocked to see that venerable sycamore, that has so long graced its midst, lying shattered and prostrate, a prey to the fierce lightning. A severe thunder-storm passed over the city in the night, which startled me greatly at the time. Little did I imagine that so illustrious a victim had fallen before its violence. Poor old tree! I could hardly refrain from tears at the sad spectacle. Few objects, indeed, were there in Nineveh more dear to its citizens, or invested with more pleasant associations. Think of the innumerable groups that, for generations, have sought shelter beneath its branches—traffickers and story-tellers, lovers and ballad-singers, limping age and frolicking childhood—and lo! in the twinkling of an eye is it thus blasted, its majestic presence, its grateful shade vanished forever. I confess I am superstitious enough to be quite unhappy about this occurrence—to see in it the anger of heaven—a portent of disasters to come. Do not laugh at me.

But I am too weary to write more; besides, little Zeresh is crying out to me to come and hear how well she can say her multiplication table. Farewell, my dear friend; the gods ever love and keep you! TELASSAR.

LETTER X.

TELASSAR TO MEMUCAN.

I GAVE you a good scolding, in my last, for your long silence. My letter had hardly been dispatched ten minutes, when yours of the 8th arrived. Since then we have received another from you, with a long postscript by Zethar, which both grieved and gratified us: the former, in telling us how long you are to be away from us, and the latter, in its many indications of the good health and spirits of the writers. And so Zethar has concluded to turn architect, and to follow in the footsteps of his excellent father. I am delighted to hear it, and wish him every success; nay, I cherish the hope that I shall yet live to compose a sonorous inscription for some great work of his, be it bridge, or aqueduct, or holy temple, that shall send his name down with honor to posterity.

The presents arrived safe, and were most acceptable. Zeresh is charmed with the fans, which are, indeed, dazzlingly beautiful, while her little namesake is equally infatuated with her apron and slippers. As for Hegai, he has done nothing but write letters, ever since the ring arrived, for the express purpose of showing the exquisite devices of its seal. The cloak has added, at least, a cubit to the stature of Semiramis, and is the envy of all the children round about. Memucan welcomed his ponies with a most enthusiastic outburst; but the crocodile's performances rather alarmed him at first. What ingenious toy-makers those Indians are! I am truly thankful to Zethar for the beautiful walking-stick. It is, indeed, a master-piece, though, as he seemed to fear, the figures at the top are somewhat gay for so demure a person as myself, and have occasioned some good-natured jokes at my expense, on the part of my collegiate brethren. Do you know I was so stupid that it was not till this morning that I discovered the superb dagger inclosed in it.

You will be pleased to hear that our learned brother, Ethan, is well again, having fully recovered from the effects of his accident. There are some traces of it on his forehead, though much slighter than I, at one time, feared. He has been to the Record-chamber daily now, for some time past, being greatly interested in the historical documents recently discovered in the old palace. He is busy preparing an analysis of their contents, a copy of which he has promised me to send you as soon as finished.

For the last few days the king has been much occupied with military affairs. Accompanied by the three princes, and a large staff, he has made his accustomed semi-annual exploration of the walls of the city, and of the four great fortresses, and I need not add, with his usual energy and thoroughness, trusting nothing to report, but examining in person every gate and tower of the metropolis. The result has been, on the whole, most satisfactory. Here and there, however, a weak spot has been detected, or an improvement suggested by his majesty, both in the city walls, and in those of the inclosures. Nay, even that master-work, the pride of Assyria, and wonder of the world, the fortress of Sennacherib itself has not yet reached the king's ideal of perfection. He has ordered several additional detached towers to be erected on the eastern side, immediately south of the Ussur; the outer ditch, connecting the two rivers, is, also, to be enlarged and deepened throughout, and the river-gate itself to be entirely reconstructed, and to be made twice as solid and lofty as the present one. This last, to my unlearned eye, seems utterly impregnable; still, as this is the point where alone an enemy, supposing him mad enough to assault the fortress, could hope to make an impression, his majesty is determined to concentrate all the resources of art upon it.

We have, also, had several parades in different quarters of the city, and a grand review of the legions by the king, in person. Of this last I saw somewhat, and was highly gratified. Never did the troops appear to more advantage; their companies all full, their equipments in perfect order, and their manœuvres performed with most creditable promptness and precision. Most pleasing of all, was the evident delight with which the presence of the king inspired them. As he rode along the lines, first on horseback, and then in his superb chariot, the shouts that rent the air had that genuine, hearty ring in them that never deceives, demonstrating, that as no monarch had ever before such lofty, and massive, and well-manned walls to protect him, so he hath, likewise, a strong-hold still more inexpugnable, in the love of his people. Prince Essarhaddon was, also, cordially greeted, evidently more so than either of his brothers.

And this leads me to speak of the only unpleasant circumstance that disturbs the general prosperity and happiness here. I know not how far the good Bel-Adon is cognizant of these affairs, and, in any event, what I say to you is in confidence. You must know, then, that an unhappy difference has arisen between his majesty and Prince Adrammelech, and in this wise: Some time since, the king imposed his commands upon the prince to take to wife the young princess of Media, the eldest and favorite daughter of King Deioces, and a maiden whom all the world report as alike beautiful and virtuous. The Median king himself is anxious to have the marriage consummated, which, indeed, every consideration of expediency seems to suggest. Who, of the allies of Assyria, so wise, so brave, so powerful, as Deioces? Who, in case of disagreement, would be so formidable an enemy? What more natural and obvious mode of conciliating the two nations, and of strengthening the foundations of the empire, than this very alliance? Unluckily, however, the prince seems to have set his heart upon one of the fair daughters of Armenia, the princess Zera—truly a lovely and discreet lady—as, strange to say, indeed, are all the children of King Milidduris, so unlike their false and weak-minded father. Now, instead of cheerfully sacrificing his desires to the commands of the king, Adrammelech has deported himself in a most ungracious, unfilial manner; not presuming openly to disobey him, he hath, yet, resorted to unworthy subterfuges, hath excused himself from visiting the Median court, on the plea of sickness, and other pretenses, greatly to the irritation of his majesty; being encouraged therein, as I, in my heart, believe, by the evil counsels of his brother, Sharezer, that dark, dangerous man, as I cannot but think him; deep, wily, ambitious, one who would stick at nothing in the way of revenging an injury, or of carrying out a guilty purpose. It grieves me to speak thus; but I have noticed many things in him of late (some of which I have alluded to in former letters to you), that compel me to this opinion. He is, indeed, the evil genius of the court, and I wish, with all my heart, that he were at the uttermost ends of the earth, at this very moment. What resistance can the credulous, easily-led Adrammelech make to a spirit so intrepid and persevering as his? And, yet, the king does not appear to mistrust him; he has never manifested the same love for him, indeed, as for his brothers; still, he has spoken to me more than once, with great warmth, of his talents, and his unquestioned ability as a soldier. How this matter will end, I know not, or how long the king's patience will hold out against such conduct. This very morning, as I was entering the chamber of audience, the prince Adrammelech hastily left it. He was very pale, and evidently much agitated. His father's brow, too, was clouded with frowns. I had hardly time to pay my homage, when he forthwith dictated a most brief and peremptory epistle to the Armenian king, ordering him instantly to bestow his daughter's hand elsewhere, under pain of his severest displeasure. Surely, this last interview must open the eyes of the prince, and make him feel the necessity of yielding to his father's will.

I received, the other day, one of the oddest, drollest letters I ever read. It was from my old friend Ophar, the judge, at Calah—the same that you called to see, you remember, on your way to Babylon, and whose eccentricities so much amused Zethar. It was in reply to some inquiries of mine, relative to the purchase of some bronzes from the sculptor Shobal—I having been long desirous to enrich my collection with a specimen or two of the works of that wonderful artist, and hoping to obtain them cheaper there than at Nineveh. His answer did by no means confine itself, however, to that subject, but discussed an infinite variety of matters, from the attempted innovation in wigs, which he is very hard upon, up to the transmigration of souls. On this last theme, he has, indeed, some of the most curious and original ideas that can be imagined; expressed as usual, with much seeming levity, and yet bearing witness to a good deal of patient and candid investigation. I cannot lay my hands upon his letter at the moment, else should I be tempted to transcribe some passages for your amusement. I read some of them to Archilochus, who was highly entertained by them. Ophar is certainly a rare humorist, and a great master of irony. The untiring enemy of all shams and affectations, he yet prefers laughing them down, to frowning them down; though he can be terribly sarcastic if he will. A literal minded person would, doubtless, be greatly mystified by many of his expressions, and a sober-minded one might justly take offense at times, at his coarseness and irreverent tone; but beneath these infirmities, we hear the beating of a kindly heart, and trace the workings of an indomitable good sense. He is now an octogenarian, and yet, he writes me, that he cannot remember having ever expended a solitary shekel upon himself, in the way of doctors' fees. With such health, can we blame him for being occasionally a little too gay and frolicksome for his years? There are certainly many judges in the realm, far more stately and dignified; but not one, I believe, who has discharged his duties with more fidelity, or whose decisions have been more uniformly wise and righteous.

Since his letter, I have received two beautiful

works of Shobal, which he bought for me—one in bronze, and the other in silver. We are all delighted with them. The former is a cup, on whose surface is represented a lonely lake, surrounded by wooded hills, and on its margin, scattered groups of deer, in every variety of attitude, done in high relief, and every figure marvelously truthful and graceful. The work in silver is a vase of exquisite finish, and beautiful proportions. On its circumference are four medallions, composed of blended fruits, flowers, and foliage, charmingly arranged, and executed with an accuracy which invites the scrutiny of the most powerful lens. Both works are, indeed, most creditable to the artist, and fully vindicate his reputation as a diligent and conscientious student of nature. I have already been offered a large advance on the price I paid for them.

* * * * *

Three days have passed since the above was written, and, oh, my friend, what sad, sad news have I to tell you! Our darling child, our sweet little Zeresh has been taken from us. Alas, alas! never more are we to behold that dear face of hers, never more to be cheered with the merry music of her voice. And, oh, the manner of her death, how sudden, how cruel! Let me briefly relate the particulars of this grievous calamity that hath overtaken us. Poor Zethar will be doubly shocked when he comes to hear them. You remember that althea-bush, that he planted for his little cousin, some three summers since, in the southern angle of the garden, directly under the nursery windows. What a beautiful one it was, so thrifty, so shapely, with such a multitude of fair flowers! How proud its little mistress was of it! This last season hath it been especially beautiful, having shot up with marvelous rapidity, till it fairly reached the level of the window-sill, and, with its host of purple-eyed blossoms, was, indeed, the admiration of all the neighbors—a flower that all delight in, and to me especially grateful, as it is the latest that blooms for us. And to think that this same treacherous tree should have been the cause of all our misery! For even so was it: one of these lovely flowers, upon the very topmost branch, caught the child's eye, and so fascinated was she by its bright hues, that she was seized with an irresistible impulse to pluck it, and, leaning from the window in her eagerness, lost her balance, and was precipitated to the ground, striking her head, as she fell, against the marble ledge of the little fountain hard-by. The poor nurse, who had had no time even to caution her against her rash attempt, rushed instantly down to her assistance; but, alas, what a sad spectacle awaited her! There lay the dear child, speechless, senseless, bleeding, her skull fractured, with her fair prize firmly clutched in her little hand. They bore her instantly within, and, in a very few moments, our good doctor was at her side; but she was past all human skill, and indeed, he only arrived in time to close her eyes. A few moans, one feeble look of seeming recognition of her dear mother, and all was over. It but adds to the keenness of our grief, to think that had she fallen in any other direction, she might very likely have been spared to us—might have escaped with a few bruises, or, at worst, a broken limb; but, oh, that fatal stone—well, well, the good gods had so ordained it, and we must bow in humble submission to their will. I need not tell you how Zeresh feels under this sudden and severe dispensation, how the children miss their poor little sister, how we all grieve for her. Who, that knew her, could help loving her? So full of winning ways and merry pranks—so intelligent, too. That very morning, she had caught me by the robe, and would not let me leave the house, till I had heard her sing the last little song she had been learning; and, oh, how prettily she warbled it! Poor bird, and shall I never listen more to thy pleasant notes? And wast thou thus doomed to perish, and for a poor flower's sake—thyself the fairest flower of all? Ah, my dear friend, how little did I imagine, when I was talking to you the other day so complacently about our family-tomb, and describing its ornaments, that it was, in a few short days, to be thus tenanted; least of all, that this pet lamb of ours would be the first to be folded within its cold embrace. But so, alas, it is! Early this morning, we consigned our dear child to her last resting-place. A few friends only were present, and the funeral rites were brief and simple. Our good priest Ammar, of the neighboring temple, made a short but fervent prayer, after which the young children of the choir chanted, with plaintive voices, the parting hymn. I wish you could have seen her, as she lay in her coffin—a sweet smile still lingering round her pretty mouth, her tiny hands folded over her bosom, a wreath of snow-white blossoms round her brow, and her little playthings at her side: a spectacle to melt the stoutest heart.

After all, there was something consoling, something poetical—was there not?—in the circumstances of her death; in the thought that she fell a victim thus to her own sweet impulses, and perished a young martyr in the cause of beauty. Perished, said I? Ah no, transplanted rather, dear bud, to far fairer climes than ours—there to blossom, and rejoice, and drink the sweet airs of heaven; flown, sweet bird, to groves far lovelier than those of earth, there to warble, the livelong day, her notes of love and praise, to the ever-blessed gods.

You are a father, my dear friend, and will not chide me for dwelling thus fondly on a father's grief. On returning to the palace, the day after our sad affliction, I was summoned to the presence of the queen, who had already heard of our bereavement, and sent a most gracious message to my dear wife, in consequence. The king, too, most kindly insisted on my returning home immediately, and excused me from all official duty, till after the funeral.

To-day I have resumed my labors, and, indeed, was but too glad to escape from my sad thoughts, amid the many documents that were awaiting my examination. Unpleasant dispatches were received yesterday from Egypt, in which King Sabaco speaks of a new and more formidable rebellion, which has broken out in Æthiopia, and earnestly invokes the assistance of Assyria, should it be necessary, to crush the insurgents. The tone and spirit of his epistle were such as to excite the respect and sympathy of the king, who, with characteristic generosity, has placed ten legions at his disposal, to be sent at such time, and to such place, as King Sabaco may designate.

Missives have also been received from our ambassador at Susa, in which he draws a frightful picture of the state of things in that metropolis—the infatuated monarch locked up in his citadel, and abandoned to all manner of debauchery; the people groaning beneath oppressive taxes; the priesthood defrauded of their revenues, and fast losing all influence in the state; the administration of justice utterly neglected—in a word, the whole affairs of the government under the control of some half dozen profligate courtiers, whose names he recites. To add to their troubles, a devastating fire hath visited some of the fairest quarters of the city, bringing infinite loss and distress in its train. Is it not grievous, that one of the loveliest spots on earth should be thus given over to misrule and ruin? The writer thinks that nothing can redeem the state from anarchy, save the deposition of the wretch who thus disgraces the holy name of king; the extermination of these base minions that minister unto his lusts; and the appointment of his son as his successor—a prince, not without parts and virtues, and to whose side, he doubts not, the people would promptly rally. How far the king will act on these statements, I cannot yet inform you. They are certainly quite too accordant with those derived from other sources. I should not be surprised if the services of our good Rabsaris should soon again be called for, and he be sent with an imposing military force to restore order to this unhappy kingdom.

On my way home this afternoon, I stopped to inquire after our invalid friend, Malech, and was told that he had at length been released from his troubles. The good man died last night, without a struggle or a groan—his last words, an expression of thankfulness that his prayers had been finally answered. Thus capricious, thus mysterious are the dealings of death! To us, he came like some midnight murderer—sudden, cruel, terrible—while this poor sufferer has been teased and mocked by him, when, for years, his fatal shaft would have been welcomed as the greatest of boons. Truly, the economy of heaven is dark: who shall presume to fathom its secrets? But I must not talk thus.

This evening we have had a visit of consolation from our dear Zethar, who spoke most kindly and seasonably. The good Ammar was also present, and, at the request of Zeresh, read aloud that sublime chapter in our sacred books, which sets forth so clearly the doctrine of immortality, and paints those wonderful pictures of the worlds beyond the grave. Never before did it sound so gloriously to me.

But no more to-night. The gods grant that my next shall have none but pleasant tidings for you. With best love to Zethar, and all our good friends in Babylon, I am your afflicted, but ever-loving

TELASSAR.

LETTER XI.

TELASSAR TO MEMUCAN.

MANY thanks, my dear friend, for your last letter. Its gracious and comforting words were most welcome to us, as were those of Zethar. I am happy to tell you that we are all well, and that our household is gradually recovering its wonted cheerfulness. Zeresh struggles bravely with her grief, and is more industrious than ever; while Semiramis is fast becoming reconciled to the loss of her little playmate and fellow-student. I wish you could see the pretty tablet which we have erected over our dear child, with its charming epitaph, composed by Archilochus.

This has been an interesting day at the palace. The king was unusually gracious and communicative, though looking, I thought, rather pale and care-worn. After the regular business of the morning had been dispatched, he introduced various topics—complaining, among other things, that he had been much annoyed of late by disagreeable dreams. "Last night especially," said he, "was I persecuted by a phantom—truly a most irreverent ghost—who loaded me with imprecations and reproaches, and denounced all manner of evil against me and mine. I will not repeat his fearful words, or recall the sad images that he caused to pass before me. Four times did this prophet of woe approach my bedside, with angry looks and attitude of menace; and what, for the moment, really startled and shocked me, was a strange resemblance, that I fancied I could trace, between his wrathful countenance and that of my own son, of Sharezer. Ah, were I as superstitious as most of my subjects—as prone to listen to these voices of the night—I should feel somewhat disquieted, perhaps insist on summoning the holy brethren, and demanding the meaning of this mysterious apparition."

Do you wonder, my friend, that I was greatly moved at these words of the king, or that, acting under the impulse of the moment, I made bold to speak freely, and to communicate my suspicions of the prince, and the grounds on which they rested? Particularly did I dwell upon that painful scene, in the corridor of the palace (of which I have before written to you, and which, indeed, I have since, not seldom, reproached myself for not disclosing to the king), wherein the prince was so devoured by guilty passion. Why that strange frenzy? Who was its object? For whose blood was he thus thirsting? Could it be that he was cherishing, even now, perhaps, some deadly hatred, ay, against his own royal father? Might there not be some feud between them, unknown to others, which yet, if unwatched, threatened dire disasters to the state? Nay, was it not the duty of his majesty, after these warnings, to convene the sacred college forthwith, and, with prayers and sacrifices, to explore the teachings of the stars, and to invoke the favor of the gods?

No; the king would not listen to the suggestion. His faith in dreams, he said, had been sorely shaken: too often had he found them false guides; too often had he been misled by the interpretations, even of the best and wisest of soothsayers. He thanked me for my loyal zeal in his behalf, and for the evident sincerity of my words; at the same time, he thought my suspicions of the prince were quite without foundation. True, that *was* an unseemly, painful exhibition that I had witnessed; and yet, what was there so strange in it after all? what on which to build such horrible conjectures? Who so discreet and virtuous, that he was not sometimes overtaken by evil passions? What breast so pure, that had not given entertainment to wicked, nay, murderous thoughts? No, no; my loyal fears were quite unfounded; there was no quarrel between him and the prince, no possible pretext for ill-will, on the part of the latter. There had never been, indeed, that warmth of love between them, that he had felt for his other children. Sharezer's was a cold, reserved nature; and yet, he had, more than once, shown himself capable of generous actions, while he had given abundant evidence of rare intelligence. Within the last few days, especially, had he been remarkably genial and communicative, both in the royal household, and in the military councils. In these last, he had spoken with so much good sense and knowledge, as to provoke the admiration of the old warrior Rabsaris himself. Indeed, the thought had occurred to the king, several times of late, that, should it be the pleasure of the gods, that Sharezer should succeed him on the throne of Assyria, he would die content, feeling that the empire would be in worthy hands.

In a word, my friend, I saw that I had spoken unadvisedly, and that all attempts to shake the faith of his majesty, in the integrity of the prince, would avail nothing. Whatever doubts might linger in my own mind, I could but acquiesce in silence. "Ah, no," added the king, after a pause, "the only thing that has annoyed me of late, in my family relations, has this day been brought to a happy issue. Read that." And he, thereupon, handed me a letter, received this morning from the prince Adrammelech, from his villa over the Tigris, in which, after excusing himself from paying his homage in person, on the score of indisposition, he speaks with grief and penitence of the past, and promises to surrender his wishes to what he is convinced are the true interests of the empire, and dutifully to pay his court to the fair princess of Media. He humbly asks, however, for a month's delay before entering on his journey—his health and spirits having been greatly impaired, he says, in consequence of the severe struggles to which his mind has thus been subjected.

I must say, I was not altogether pleased with the tone of this letter. It seemed artificial and constrained, and I was even uncharitable enough to see some stratagem lurking beneath it; what, I know not, and I trust, the creation merely of my jealous fears. His majesty, however, was evidently satisfied, and relieved by it. He commanded me to read it over to him aloud, and presently dictated a most gracious and loving answer. It was hardly finished when there were received dispatches from the Persian court, of a very interesting nature. I mentioned to you, in my last, the frightful condition of affairs in that unlucky kingdom. A most favorable change has since taken place, however, and much sooner than was anticipated. It seems that for more than a month past, the king has utterly neglected all his duties, religious and political, and abandoned himself to the most reckless intemperance, till, at length, the patience of the gods has been exhausted, and a brain-fever has carried off the wretch in the midst of his debauchery. The particulars of his death are minutely recited, but the details are altogether too loathsome to be repeated. In this crisis, his son, with most commendable courage and promptness, has seized the reins of government, and has been received with acclamations, by both army and people. Anticipating any adverse action on the part of the conspirators, who had been mainly instrumental in thus brutalizing his father, and involving the nation in disgrace and suffering, he has chopped off their heads in the most quiet and summary manner. Three hours, indeed, had not elapsed since the death of his predecessor, when a score of ill-favored countenances, of the more notorious of these profligates, were seen grinning on pikes from the battlements of the palace, to the unbounded delight of the multitude. With the same energy has he set about reforming abuses, and relieving the distresses of his people. This is the substance of the dispatches received from our ambassador, the contents of which were most acceptable to his majesty. This day has a courier been sent to the new monarch, with missives expressive of the king's approbation of his proceedings; excusing him, moreover, from the payment of all tribute for the coming year, and offering him such aid, or counsel, as he may need, towards the better establishment of his authority.

After the audience, as I was crossing the western court, on my way to the Archive-chamber, I met the princes Sharezer and Essarhaddon. The former took pains to stop me, and made me a long speech. It was most gratifying to him, he said, to find how high I stood in the esteem of his royal father, and to witness the fidelity and zeal with which my duties, public and private, were discharged. But I must not, in my loyal love, neglect the claims of my own health, or those of my dear family. My life was altogether too valuable a one to the empire, to be thus put in jeopardy by so unremitting a devotion to my various labors: (with other remarks of a kindred nature). The gods forgive me for my unjust suspicions, but not a syllable of this same prettily composed discourse seemed to me to come from the heart of the speaker. Nay, I even fancied that I could detect in it a latent tone of sarcasm and malice, prophetic of coming evil. This mistrust sufficiently betrayed itself, in my stiff and formal acknowledgments to the prince for his good opinion; but he affected not to see it, and was most profuse in his gracious expressions as we parted. *Am* I wrong in my suspicions of this man? If I know myself, I am not prompt to spy mischief in my brethren, or fond of exploring the evil parts of poor human nature; but so it is; there is something about Sharezer that involuntarily inspires me with uneasiness and alarm, and I was but too happy to be released from his odious presence. Oh, how different from his cordial, truthful, charming brother, Essarhaddon! A prince among ten thousand. Who does not love his playful wit, his genial humor? He has honored me with his company several times of late, both in the Record-chamber, and once or twice at my own house. We had a long talk together the other day, in the new study, which, by the way, he admires vastly. Zeresh, who was present a part of the time, was enchanted with him; and as for Semiramis, he has completely won her heart, by a plaything which he brought her, namely, a pet dog, and one of the tiniest, drollest creatures I ever beheld. I should think it hardly weighed a pound, collar, bells, and all. It is short-haired, and of a jet-black throughout, with the exception of a small white spot on the tip of its nose, which has a very funny appearance. Its eyes shine like two little sparks. It is of Theban origin, highly educated, and very dainty in its tastes. Among its many accomplishments, it has a most peculiar mode of hopping about on its hind legs, producing an effect so comical that Zeresh herself could not resist it. Poor thing! it was her first real hearty laugh since our dear child left us. I wish you could have seen the look of mingled astonishment and pity on the face of our veteran Rough, when the new-comer was presented to him. It was a droll interview, and, had I your ready pencil, I should be tempted to reproduce it for your edification. I offer no apology, my dear friend, for entering into these details; for, after all, what theme is there more worthy, or spectacle more edifying, than the innocent joys of one's children.

The young Prince of Lydia has arrived at last, having traveled very leisurely. He spent several days at Opis and at Dura, and also at Rehoboth, at which last city he was entertained, among others, by our friend, the invalid colonel, whose health, I am happy to hear, is mending fast. He has apartments in the palace, where I have had the honor of being presented to him. I found him even more handsome and intelligent than your description had prepared me to expect, and, certainly, a most striking likeness of his illustrious father—as he was, at least, when I saw him, more than twenty years ago (dear me, how time flies), when I, too, was a youthful traveler in western Asia. The prince had much to say of his Babylonian experiences, and of the kindness of King Bel-Adon. Nor was your name forgotten. He spoke with great enthusiasm of your architectural labors. I was quite delighted with the earnest way in which he said: "I would rather have the glory of designing such a palace than wear the crowns of all the kingdoms of the earth." Nor was this a mere outburst of unthinking admiration; for he described its characteristic features with a precision which showed that he has already found time to become a faithful art-student. I did not, of course, venture to allude to his family relations. He himself, however, of his own accord related several facts concerning his good father, which much interested me; more especially, in illustration of his religious ardor—an element in his character which was quite marked when I was a visitor at his court. Since the queen's death, however, (now nearly five years), this trait has been far more strikingly developed than ever. Without neglecting the interests of his kingdom, he has yet abandoned forever all ideas of earthly conquests and renown, and devotes every thought and moment that he can command to the service of the gods; performing pilgrimages, building and restoring temples, reviving holy days and usages, sending precious offerings to all the shrines and oracles of his own and of other states, these are the occupations dearest to his heart; and, indeed, his pious munificence has become a proverb throughout Lydia, and all the regions round about. The recent unhappy events in his family have more than ever disgusted him with the vain shows and guilty passions of life. Were he to consult his own feelings merely, he would straightway abandon the cares of state, and devote the remainder of his days to prayer and meditation. Indeed, the prince suggested that one great motive which his father had, in sending him upon his travels, was that he might be the better enabled to discharge the duties of monarch, on his return, in the event of the abdication of Gyges. This explanation certainly varies somewhat from, though by no means irreconcilable with, that given in the king's own letters, as referred to by you. I noticed, of course, those occasional fits of abstraction and pensiveness of which you speak; but they were mere fleeting shadows, and will, I trust, soon disappear altogether before the genial influences of travel. I was much gratified, by the way, at hearing the beautiful tribute which Prince Ardys paid to his mother's memory. She was truly a remarkable woman, combining as she did, such unflinching courage and energy of will, with so many sweet and winning ways. You have more than once heard me speak of her beauty, and of the deep impression it made upon me.

Our guest proposes to spend about a month in the metropolis. To-day he has been exploring the splendors of the new temple. This evening he is to be the guest of our good general, who has honored me with an invitation to meet him; while to-morrow there is to be a magnificent entertainment in his honor, at the palace of Sargon.

Since writing the above, I have had the misfortune to sprain my ankle. Day before yesterday it happened, as I was alighting from my mule before my own door. My mind was wandering at the time, or I should have been more circumspect. The truth is, I had just come from your house, where I wished to see how our friend Elath was coming on in his new quarters. I found him quite delighted with them, and everything about the house and garden in perfect order. On taking leave of him, your image naturally claimed possession of my thoughts, and I was looking forward fondly to the time when you and Zethar should be restored to us again, safe and sound, in your old homestead, and your talents employed in the service of the king. Nay, I had even selected, in my mind, the site for the palace, with which you were to adorn your native city, had arranged its plan and proportions, and was in the very act of rearing the stately columns that were to grace its eastern front, when my beast suddenly stopped, and, being thus taken by surprise, and dismounting rather hastily, my foot became entangled somehow in my robe, and down I came pretty heavily to the ground. I was afraid, at first, that I had hurt my head badly, but fortunately escaped with a few bruises and the above-mentioned sprained ankle. The faithful Eno was at his post, as usual, and picked me up instantly. For a moment, Zeresh was quite overcome, but soon regained her tranquillity. The accident has occasioned me some little pain and annoyance, and has, moreover, interfered somewhat with my duties at the palace, as it will for a day or two longer. Luckily, though, it is a week of comparative leisure, and I shall not be so much missed. But the next will be a very busy one, as the thirteenth year of his majesty's reign is fast approaching its completion, and I have to prepare the materials for the accustomed annual inscription. The tablet is to be erected in the new temple, being the first of the new series, and it is the king's wish to have it as full and accurate as possible. I need not tell you how much hard labor is implied in the faithful discharge of this duty; how many reports I have to read, returns to examine, wearisome columns of figures to go over. The items of the revenue alone, how many and various! Tolls, taxes, tributes, tithes, rents, reversions, forfeitures, spoils of war, and gifts of peace; these, under their various heads—religious, military, legal, commercial—it is, of course, my province to investigate, and to systematize; faithfully to collect, and truly to set forth the facts. Besides all which, and much more kindred labor, as you are aware, the remarkable events of the year are to be recited, clearly and succinctly, and in chronological order. You would pity me, indeed, could you see the myriad documents through which I have to plod my weary way, in compiling these statistics; and some of them by no means models, either in the way of arrangement or of calligraphy. Still I must not be understood as complaining; on the contrary, I fully appreciate the dignity and importance of such a trust, and the glorious truths which these same statements embody; these shining witnesses to the resources and splendors of the empire, that are to be thus reared in holy places, and to be read with admiration and gratitude by the long generations that are to come after us.

Yesterday was my dear wife's birthday, and, though we did not spend it in the usual joyous manner, and, though our tears flowed afresh for our poor little Zeresh, still, on the whole, it was a pleasant anniversary. Nor did our good friends forget us. Many kind messages and presents were received: among them, a superb pair of ear-rings from Zethar, with which Zeresh was delighted; very large and massive, the gold beautifully sculptured, and the rubies the most brilliant I ever saw. They were none the less welcome, I assure you, when we were told that they were fashioned after a design furnished by yourself. The good Menahem remembered us likewise, though in a manner, as it seemed to me, more characteristic of the donor, than appropriate to the occasion; two little, snow-white pigs being the evidences of his appreciation of my wife's many virtues. A very long and curious letter accompanied the porklings, in which the particulars of their birth and breeding, and an enumeration of the shining qualities which had illustrated their brief lives, were given with great minuteness. The writer then proceeded to issue his instructions as to the only proper mode of serving up the creatures. I shall not transcribe them for your benefit, though they were characterized by great earnestness, solemnity, and copiousness of detail. For a wonder, our old cook was amiable and docile enough to act in accordance with them, and the result was a triumphant one. Generally I have rather an Egyptian aversion to these animals, but the locust-sauce (the *only* sauce, M. says, which should *ever* be allowed to approach them), had a piquancy about it, which was quite irresistible. Poor Menahem, I fear that, if the truth were told, his heart is far more in the market-place than in the temple; and that the appearance of a new dish upon his table would impress him far more deeply than that of a new planet in the heavens.

To-day, I am much better, and have hobbled about the house somewhat; and have, also, with the assistance of Hegai, who has kindly devoted himself to me for the last three days, put my library to rights, which, truth to say, it sadly needed. Since you saw it, it has received some valuable additions, both manuscripts and tablets. Many of them are the fruits of the recent excavations, and were presented to me by his majesty. Some of the tablets are quite large, and admirably preserved—the forms of the letters being as perfect, and the impressions of the seals as fresh, as if they had just been taken out of the furnace. One of them interested me greatly. It bears date the fourth year of the reign of King Adrammelech the First (just three hundred and twenty-seven years ago) and is an authenticated copy of a deed of gift from that monarch, to one Mardan, of Calah, in consideration of distinguished services rendered by him in a campaign against the Syrians, of the identical tract of ground on which my own house and gardens are situated. The description of the property corresponds, almost word for word, with that in the deed executed eighty years since, by Albon, the then owner, in favor of my paternal grandfather. The property had then been sixty years in the possession of the family of Albon, beyond which time the title cannot be traced. Since this discovery, I confess, I have been quite curious to recover the lost links of the chain, and to know something more of the gallant soldier who was thus signally honored by his king. There are two or three families bearing his name, now living in the metropolis, but they are all, without exception, obscure and illiterate persons. As a last resort, I have written to our good judge, to see if he cannot find some glimmerings of light on this subject among the records of Calah. After all, however, this is a matter of mere personal interest. Many of the tablets are much older than the above, and of undoubted historical value. I have not yet found time faithfully to examine them, but our friend, Ethan, has explored them with evident delight, and I must refer you to his elaborate description of the late discoveries, which, he says, will be completed about the end of the month. My collection has, also, been enriched lately, with a superb set of medallions, in bronze, illustrative of the recent Armenian campaign. These, too, were a gift from the king, being copied from the new sculptures in the palace.

Speaking of manuscripts, there are none, my dear friend, in my library, that I set more store by than your own letters. I have now nearly three hundred of them, all carefully arranged in the order of time, from boyhood up. Some few of these last, Hegai and I looked over, and were greatly amused, both with the text, and with the extraordinary figures in the margin; even droller, I think, than any of Zethar's. And, yet, under all the fun and mischief, I fancy I can trace, from the very beginning, indications of that fondness for art, and that spirit of patient investigation, which have so characterized the writer in after-life. Dear me, is it possible that more than forty years have rolled by since we first exchanged pot-hooks?

In addition to these employments, Zeresh has been kind enough to read to me an hour or two each day, both in prose and verse; the former, mainly from that quaint and charming volume that you admire so greatly, Sanchoniatho's History of Phœnicia; the latter, from a collection of hymns, transcribed by the pious Ammar, from the originals in the library of the Archimagus. Many of these were quite new to me, and very beautiful. Nor did their beauties suffer aught at the hands of the dear reader.

This morning, I received a pleasant little note from prince Essarhaddon, in his usual playful, cordial vein. Accompanying it was a magnificent bouquet for my wife, and a very funny letter, addressed to Semiramis. He is to honor me with a visit to-morrow, and would have called upon me sooner, but his time has been pretty much taken up with our illustrious visitor from Lydia.

The crowning event of the day, however, has been a visit from the good Clœlius, who has just returned from his embassy to Media. I was right glad to embrace our friend once more, I assure you. He is looking in fine health, and speaks with great enthusiasm of his journey. He was most graciously received by the king, who seems, indeed, to have taken an especial fancy to him, and to have quite pretermitted the usual rigorous etiquette of his court on this occasion; not merely treating him as a familiar friend, but absolutely making him sit by his side while administering justice. With this spectacle, Clœlius (who, by the way, has wonderfully improved in his Assyrian) was much impressed; the equity and promptness of the king's decisions, and his ingenious devices for extorting the truth from reluctant witnesses, were, indeed, worthy of all praise. His majesty, it seems, was not unfamiliar with the virtues of good King Numa, and has sent him, by his ambassador, many evidences of his regard; the most remarkable among them being a copy of the code and of the creed of the divine Zoroaster, executed in letters of gold, on tablets of ivory, with borders of exceeding richness. Truly, a magnificent and, in this case, most appropriate gift. Clœlius has promised to show it to me before he leaves.

Of the beautiful capital of Media, our friend spoke as all travelers speak. The far-glittering Ecbatana, with its rainbow-hued walls, and gilded battlements, and central crowning palace, rising stately from the plain, with its girdle of gardens, and background of noble mountains, was, indeed a picture whose varied charms could never be effaced from the memory of the beholder. And then its clear skies, and invigorating breezes: true, an occasional keen blast from the northwest would recall the more genial warmth of Nineveh, but he could not imagine a spot on earth more attractive, when arrayed in the glories of summer. In reply to my inquiries, Clœlius gave a glowing account of the charms of the young princess—that fortunate lady, so soon to be the blessed means of establishing anew the friendship of the two monarchs. Nor was she less intelligent than beautiful. He had been honored with several interviews with her, and her remarks showed how much she had profited by the instructions of her august father.

I am afraid that you will not have the pleasure of seeing our friend at Babylon. The period assigned to his mission has already expired, and his duties summon him homeward. He is, moreover, quite impatient to embrace once more his dear wife and children. We were much gratified to find that he had not forgotten our little lost one, and with his kind words of sympathy, on hearing of our bereavement.

To-morrow I hope to be strong enough to walk as far as your house, and the day after to resume my accustomed labors. On looking over my diary, I find that it is exactly six months to-day since you and Zethar left us. And a lovely day it has been, too. The spring is fast returning upon us with all its gracious attributes ; the flowers are again peeping forth, and the pleasant notes of the ring-doves once more greet our ears. How I wished for you, this evening, as we sat in our porch enjoying the beautiful sunset. Well, well, the gods know best what is good for us. That they may bless you with many happy years, and a serene old age, and a tranquil dismissal at last, is the heart's wish of your ever loving TELASSAR.

LETTER XII.

TELASSAR TO MEMUCAN.

Oh, my friend, what a task is before me! What a dark page am I about to unfold to you! Three days have passed since this terrible calamity that hath befallen us, and not till now have I been able sufficiently to regain my tranquillity, and to collect my thoughts, in order to write you about it. You will have heard the sad tale, long ere this reaches you; still, I must endeavor to give you now, calmly as I may, a more minute and connected account of this cruel, cruel visitation. Yes, just three days, this very afternoon, since I took leave of our good king—a last leave on earth. Oh, to think that I shall never more behold the light of that glorious countenance—never more render my grateful homage! But, who shall question the decrees of heaven? The day had been quite a busy and interesting one at the palace, and I had spent a large part of it in the presence of his majesty, reading dispatches, writing from his dictation, and also submitting to his inspection various documents which I had prepared, and the contents of which gave him evident satisfaction. He was graciously pleased to express, not only his delight at the prosperous state of affairs to which they bore witness, but likewise his approbation of the pains-taking fidelity evinced in their preparation (and, to say truth, they had cost me many weary hours), and that my labors should not be forgotten or unrewarded: meanwhile, I must receive this token of his esteem. Therewith, he put upon my finger a superb ring, blazing with sapphires. Ere I had time to stammer out my thanks for this beautiful gift, he added: "But methinks, Telassar, in your eagerness to set forth the whole truth, you have multiplied words somewhat unnecessarily here, and that some of these statements might have been abbreviated to advantage. And, while I am finding fault, I must say that you are, at times, a little too nice about trifles, and, moreover, somewhat uncharitable in your interpretation of motives." (This last was a manifest allusion to that most unlucky speech of mine, in reference to the Prince Sharezer, about which I wrote you.) "Do not, however," he kindly added, "be downhearted: we are all liable to errors of judgment, and far worse offenses might be pardoned to a love so loyal as yours." He then went on to speak of the bright aspect of the future and of the many enjoyments, the gods willing, yet in store for him, both as a king and as a father. In a very few days, the Prince Adrammelech would depart for Media, soon to return with his fair betrothed, and we must see to it that this so joyous an event should be celebrated with becoming magnificence. Prince Sharezer would probably take command of the army destined for Egypt; if, indeed, King Sabaco should require its aid, which he yet trusted might not be the case. All would depend, however, on the tenor of the next dispatches. His majesty then remarked, and with unusual warmth and tenderness of manner, how delightful were these intervals of repose from the pomps and cares of state—so many of which the gods had kindly accorded him of late—these blessed retreats in the bosom of one's family, and of the pleasure with which he looked forward to meeting his queen and children, at the royal banquet, that evening. He then spoke of some superb cedars which had caught his eye, the day before, while riding in the Royal Park, and which he thought of having transplanted, as a most becoming and appropriate border for the tower of Sardanapalus, now fast rising to completion. Afterwards he alluded to our good friend from Rome, who has since left us, and to a robe which I must see before returning home, and which he designed as a gift to King Numa—a magnificent fabric of gold and purple, many of the devices of which were the work of the hands of the young princess. The last words he ever uttered to me were, when, summoning me to one of the windows of the audience-chamber, he bade me gaze on the gorgeous sunset which was then illuminating the west. It was, indeed, a picture of radiant and unmatchable beauty. And, oh, to think that this was the last time on earth that our good king was to enjoy its splendors, the last time that he was to pay his adoration to the blessed god then smiling upon us; to whom he, of all mortals, had rendered most signal honor: in whose name he had so lately reared the most magnificent of earthly temples. Oh, to be thus suddenly, cruelly removed from all this pomp and beauty, to the cold, dark chamber of death! How bitter, how crushing the thought, but for our faith in brighter worlds to come! After lingering many moments in silence over the superb spectacle, the king, with a most cordial farewell, graciously dismissed me.

Do you wonder, my dear friend, that I linger thus fondly and minutely over these particulars of our final interview? With what a joyous, grateful heart did I ride home that evening, and how delighted was the good Zeresh to hear my report of the king's words, and to behold the sparkling ring, the precious token of his approbation.

The next morning, immediately after our morning meal, as I was sitting, my wife by my side, listening to our little daughter, who *would* insist on my hearing her spelling-lesson, suddenly I raised my eyes, and whom should I behold but Zethar, who had just alighted from his horse, and was entering the garden-gate? As he hastily approached the house, I could not but notice that he was greatly agitated, and that his countenance betokened some most unpleasant news for us. Going forth, I met him in the porch. He was trembling violently. Seizing me by the robe, he said, in low, hurried tones: "Oh, Telassar, such tidings, such tidings—"

"Compose yourself, my dear friend, what is it?"

"Our king, our gracious king—"

"Speak, speak, I beseech you."

"Has been murdered, cruelly murdered, this very morning, in the temple of Ashur—ay, in the very act of paying his vows to--

"And the assassins?"

"Have fled, no man knows whither. But come, there is not a moment to be lost: to the palace! to the palace!"

Fortunately my beast was already saddled and

at the door, and I had barely time to repeat the terrible news to poor Zeresh, who, in her anxiety, had followed me to the porch, and we departed. In spite of all our haste, however, it was more than an hour before we reached the eastern stair-case of the platform, so obstructed were the streets—the horsemen flying in all directions, the scattered groups of terrified listeners, everything bearing fearful witness to the truth of Zethar's story. Alighting, we with great difficulty forced our way up the stair-case, through the dense throng of men, women, and children, whom the troops were vainly striving to repel from the portals of the palace. Reaching the top, at last, we were recognized by the guard, and straightway conducted through the gates, and to the chamber of audience. Here we found Prince Essarhaddon, and our good archimagus, with two other members of the holy college. The prince was pacing the room in great agitation. As we entered, he turned, and thanked us for our prompt obedience to his summons. (It seems that we had already been sent for, though the messenger had passed us on the way: as, indeed, were all the fathers of the sacred college, and the commanders of the legions.) Our presence, he added, and counsel were, truly, most needful in this terrible crisis. "But your brothers, the princes?" I asked. Oh, my friend, I shall never forget the expression of the prince's face, at that moment—the look of mingled horror and grief, with which alone he replied to my question. At once, the fatal truth seemed to flash upon me. And yet, it could not, could not be. But this suspense was not to be endured, and I earnestly besought his grace to relieve our minds, and to reveal to us the sad details of this dire calamity. In response to this appeal, he had not the heart, he said, to rehearse the story, but referred us to the archimagus. Whereupon the good man took us aside, and, in hurried words, and with ill-suppressed emotion, told us the few and fearful facts that have yet come to light, concerning this foul crime.

It appears that shortly after sunrise, the king, accompanied by the princes Adrammelech and Sharezer, and attended by his parasol-bearer, and four spearmen of the guard, went to offer up his accustomed morning prayers at the temple of Ashur. Ordinarily, as you are aware, his majesty goes without attendance, and by the private covered way which connects the temple and the palace. Still, not unfrequently, and especially in these lovely mornings of spring, he prefers the usual public entrance. On reaching the temple, he and the princes at once withdrew behind the curtain which separates the chapel, set apart for the royal family, from the rest of the inner court—the attendants being stationed in waiting, as usual, at the central portal. A good half-hour had elapsed when the princes came forth from the chapel, the Prince Sharezer saying to the bearer of the parasol that his majesty had expressed a wish to be left alone, and that on no account must his devotions be disturbed. With this the princes departed. The attendant noticed that Prince Adrammelech was quite pale, and seemingly agitated about something; still the circumstance made but little impression on him at the moment. And now the dial in the outer court indicated that another half-hour had passed, and those in waiting began to be anxious. Surely this was very strange—these protracted prayers, this long absence from the palace—on the part, too, of one so proverbially prompt and methodical in all things as his majesty. What could it mean? Might he not have been overtaken by some sudden illness? Or, lost in thought, perhaps, may he not have returned by the private passage, and neglected to instruct them accordingly? Still they waited a few moments longer, and then the attendant, trembling, and not without strange forebodings, approached the curtain, and drawing it gently aside, what a spectacle met his eyes! Prostrate, at the foot of the altar, there lay our gracious king, dead—quite dead—his garments steeped in gore—the blood still trickling from the fatal wound. One hand convulsively grasped his robe, the other was seemingly in search of his dagger. One wound alone was found upon his person; a single blow, aimed with unerring, deadly malice, had straightway pierced his heart. Your own imagination, my friend, must fill up the details of this terrible scene; the horror and outcry of the attendants, the lamentations of the priests, who came thronging in from the chambers of the outer court, the wild excitement of the people and the soldiers, as the news was borne along to the palace, and through all the quarters of the city—the wail of the women, the frantic grief of the poor queen, the distraction of Prince Essarhaddon, and the bitterness of his anguish, when confronted with this sad spectacle. Soon recovering himself, however, he showed an energy worthy indeed of his august father. With all due dispatch and secresy was the body borne back to the palace, to the private apartment of the queen, where it now lay. Messengers were immediately sent to summon the holy fathers, and the generals of the legions, and likewise to all the gates of the city, with strict orders that no man should issue forth. "And here, my friends," said the good archimagus, "we see on what slight contingencies the gods sometimes cause the weightiest events of life to depend. It so happened that this was the very first morning, for many days, that the prince had not accompanied his father and brothers to the temple. A raging tooth, it seems, had deprived him of his night's rest, and, in consequence, he had not risen at his usual early hour. Oh, *had* he been present in the chapel, can we believe that this fearful crime would have been consummated; or, at least, would not the alarm have been given, and these accursed traitors and parricides been, ere this, in the hands of the executioners? But we must not call in question the wisdom of the gods, who will yet deliver these wretches into our power."

Such is the substance of the good man's narrative. He had hardly finished it, when messengers arrived with the news that the two princes had been seen riding forth from the Armenian gate, about an hour, indeed, before the orders arrived closing it against all egress. A large body of horse was instantly sent in pursuit of the fugitives; but, up to this time, now nearly three days, they have not returned. And here let me briefly state all that is yet known of the murderers. It appears that they went back immediately from the temple to the palace, and that Prince Sharezer ordered their horses to be got ready forthwith, and to wait for them at the foot of the southern stair-case. Meanwhile the princes went to the officer on duty in the audience-chamber, to whom prince Sharezer remarked that his majesty had instructed him to say, that he need not be expected at the palace for some time yet, as he had some special instructions to give to the chief-priest, in relation to the affairs of the temple. He added that the prince Adrammelech and himself were about to ride as far as the newly-restored tower, where they would be found, or in that immediate neighborhood, in case the king should require their presence at the palace. No sooner were they out of sight, however, but they must have taken a precisely opposite direction, and were last seen, as above stated, issuing forth from the city, on the road to Armenia. Whether they have sought some hiding-place, where they have thus far eluded the vigilance of their pursuers, or, as is more probable, have traveled with such speed as to have reached the frontier before being overtaken, and have thrown themselves upon the protection of the Armenian court—these points, a day or two, at furthest, must determine. In the latter event, one thing is certain, that that pusillanimous, false-hearted monarch will be guided solely by his own selfish fears, in his treatment of them. But to return to the palace. It was not long ere the rest of the holy fathers, and Rabsaris, and the other generals made their appearance. At the prince's request, a solemn council was immediately held, wherein, after brief consultation, it was found to be the unanimous and earnest wish of all, that he should, at once, receive our homage, as the new sovereign, and then, without delay, assuming his robes of state, present himself to the soldiers, and to the excited multitude without. This suggestion was promptly complied with; whereupon, followed by us all, the prince made his appearance in the balcony, directly over the central portal of the eastern front of the palace. I need not tell you, my friend, how well his royal attire became him, or of the noble expression of blended dignity and sorrow upon his beautiful countenance, or of the effect which his presence produced upon the people. A moment's breathless pause, and the air was rent with acclamations. Silence again restored, our good Rabsaris, at the king's command, spoke a few words to the multitude—thanking them, in the name of the new monarch, for these expressions of their confidence and love; stating that a proclamation would be published ere set of sun, and distributed throughout the city, setting forth the circumstances of the death of his royal father, and the time and manner of such propitiatory offerings to the gods as should be appointed by the sacred college; finally, commanding them to retire at once, and peacefully, to their respective homes. Again the people shouted, and then, with cheerful promptness, obeyed the royal mandate. In a very few moments, tranquillity reigned once more, within and around the palace. After our return to the audience-chamber, as I was about to take leave of his majesty, he stopped me, and was graciously pleased to say, that I must consider myself as holding the same relations, both friendly and official, towards himself, as I had held towards his father; and, moreover, that my services must be put into instant requisition. Appropriate dispatches must be sent off, that very day, to all the capitals of the tributary kingdoms; and first of all, a most plain and peremptory one, to the court of Armenia, whose faithless monarch, he greatly feared, had some secret understanding with these wretched murderers. Accordingly, after giving some instructions to Rabsaris, and a few moments' consultation with the archimagus, he proceeded to dictate these various epistles, and likewise a proclamation—a copy of which I shall send you with this letter. The night was far spent ere I was released from my labors, and reached once more my own quiet home.

Such, my friend, were the events of this fatal, memorable day; such the circumstances, few, indeed, and enveloped in mystery, of this most atrocious murder, which, I need not say, is still the all-absorbing topic of our thoughts. The place where it occurred, the relations of the parties, the seeming want of all motive for committing it, the apparent absence of all accomplices, the reckless risks incurred by its perpetrators, the cruel, fatal blow itself, and, above all, the marvelous presence of mind and audacious falsehoods of Prince Sharezer, after the deed was done—all these things surround it with a terror and a malignity that bewilder our understandings, as much as they appall our hearts. *Are* these things so? Is it not some wild, hideous dream that I am describing to you? Alas, let yon desolate palace answer—these silent streets, these woe-stricken faces, these temples thronged with mourners, these lamentations that, even as I write, pierce the ear!

In vain, my friend, do I seek to read this fearful riddle. That the mad, wicked ambition of Prince Sharezer is at the bottom of this crime; that he has long cherished murderous thoughts, aimed at the life of our good king; that Prince Adrammelech has been a mere creature in his hands: these things who can doubt? But to select such a spot and time for the murder, to make no provision for the fearful perils with which the attempt was environed, to derive no advantage, that we can trace, from its sucessful consummation, such conduct as this, on the part of the crafty Sharezer, stands not within the prospect of belief. What, then, *are* we to believe? That some accursed inspiration of the evil one suddenly possessed him, ay, while in the very act of prayer, that instantly obeying the hellish impulse, he rushed, with drawn dagger, upon the poor king, bending, absorbed in pious thoughts; that he thus took him utterly by surprise, with no opportunity to struggle, or even to cry for help; that the rash deed once done, the native courage and dissimulation of the murderer soon came to his assistance; that he easily compelled the terror-stricken Adrammelech into silent acquiescence; and that he then contrived those cunning falsehoods, in order to throw the attendants off their guard, and so open the door for their escape? Does this sound like the truth? Does it afford any clue to this terrible mystery? I know not what to think, nor, indeed, have I the heart to speculate further upon the subject. Time alone can reveal these guilty secrets; time, and the confessions of these wretched parricides, whom surely the gods will not suffer to escape us. One thought cheers us greatly in our affliction

—that neither in the court, nor in the city, have any partners in their guilt been found. Three days have passed, and there is not a man within the walls of Nineveh, that I have heard of, against whom the finger of suspicion has been raised. Whatever the ultimate designs of the traitors may have been, and to whatever quarter they may have looked for aid, they dared not tamper with the loyalty of their fellow-townsmen. What a tribute is this, my dear friend, to the virtues of our good king; what a testimony to the universal, heart-felt love of his people!

The day following the murder, after my official labors were completed, I was graciously permitted by his majesty to look upon the countenance of my royal master as he lay in death. Oh the sadness, the pallor of that face! Oh, how different from that sweet smile that played across it, when I last beheld it. And yet, how serene in its sadness! How majestic in its repose! How, my friend, can I describe the thoughts that rushed through my mind, as I lingered fondly over it? Oh, *can* it be, that thou hast been snatched away from us, forever, thus suddenly, thus cruelly, and by the hands of thy unnatural children? Now, in the height of thy glory, the perfection of thy powers, thy mind more than ever filled with magnificent conceptions, thy heart with holy, loving thoughts. Farewell, farewell, king, benefactor, father! Let others speak of thy mighty conquests, thy world-wide sway; of the terrors of thy wars, and the splendors of thy triumphs; let the holy brethren and the singers, with prayers and hymns, set forth thy virtues, and our sorrows; let thy glorious works, throughout the land, and this thy chosen city, filled with the tokens of thy munificence, proclaim thee worthily to the long ages that are to come; let the sculptors multiply everywhere thy divine image, and the historians proudly inscribe, on the tablets of temples and palaces, thy mighty name and attributes: but unto me, thy faithful, loving servant, far more dear and precious is the remembrance, not of the high priest, and of the monarch, but of the man, the husband, father, benefactor! Oh, can I ever forget thy gracious smile, the music of thy voice, thy genial wit, thy searching wisdom, thine eye, fierce and terrible, indeed, in its anger; but unto me ever beaming with benignant light? But alas, that light is forever darkened. Thou art gone —gone from the midst of thy faithful people; translated to brighter worlds, and to the company of the blessed gods; there still to watch over us; to be our advocate with the Holy Twelve, and with Him, the Father of Nations!—ay, there to receive our pious vows and solemn worship, as when on earth, our loving homage! But I must not dwell longer on thoughts which, my friend, I know will find a faithful echo in your loyal heart.

To-morrow the embalmers will begin their labors; and in a few days, the time and manner of the funeral pageant will be duly proclaimed to the people. It is the wish of the king, that his father's body should be deposited in that tower which his pious zeal had so nearly restored; and, indeed, what more magnificent, or appropriate monument could be devised?

Oh, with what impatience are we waiting to hear of the capture of these wretched traitors! I shall not fail to write you, the very instant we hear of their delivery into our hands; unless, indeed, they should anticipate, by self-slaughter, the terrible punishment that awaits them.

But I am weary, and must seek repose. I cannot tell you how much I have suffered, both in mind and body, from the excitements and fatigues of the last three days. Farewell, my dear friend. The gods ever bless thee and thine. TELASSAR.

www.ingramcontent.com/pod-product-compliance
Lightning Source LLC
LaVergne TN
LVHW050518100826
845148LV00002B/372

* 9 7 8 1 4 2 5 5 2 0 6 0 1 *